A Preacher's Path:
A Tale Of Redemption

Special Thanks

To all the readers of this book, thank you for taking the time to immerse yourselves in these words. Your support and curiosity mean the world to me.
As you turn these pages, I hope you find inspiration and joy in every story, and have as much fun reading this book as i had writing it. Remember, with God, all things are possible. Let this truth guide you in your journey, encouraging you to embrace challenges and pursue your dreams with faith and determination.
Thank you for being a part of this adventure!

Dedication

To my beloved wife, Kelly, whose unwavering love and support illuminate my path. You are the heart of our family, and every word in this book carries the essence of your strength and grace. Not a day goes by that I don't thank God for you. You truly are the heart and soul of this book my very own "Michelle". I love you sweetheart.

To our ten incredible children—Joanna, Lilly, Maddy, Adrienne, Tay, Alley, Gabby, Garrett, Jonah, and Noah. Each of you brings a unique light into our lives, inspiring me every day with your laughter, curiosity, and boundless love. This book is a reflection of our journey together, a testament to the beautiful chaos and joy that fills our home, and the

unstoppable and unwavering love I have for each of you. Last but certainly not least Jamie, the newest addition to our family. I know it's only been a short while that you have been with us , but I just want you know what a joy and honor it has been to get to know you and have you be a part of our lives. I know you haven't heard this often but " I Love You Son" and I'm proud of the man you are becoming.

May our stories continue to intertwine, and may we always cherish the moments we share.

With all my love,

Cody("Big Daddy")Wright -A.K.A. "Pops"

Table of Contents:

Foreward

In a land where the sun scorches the earth and the wind
whispers tales of old, there lies a story that intertwines the
threads of history, redemption, and unexpected laughter.
This book invites you to journey
Alongside a preacher-turned-gunslinger, a man whose faith
is tested in the most extraordinary of ways. After the tragic
murder of his family, he finds himself on a relentless quest
not only for vengeance but also for the love he thought
lost forever, upon discovering that three of his children
survived the horrific attack.
As he rides into the unknown, he encounters the stark
realities of a world where justice is often as elusive as a
desert mirage. Yet, amid the shadows of his past and the
weight of his grief, he is joined by two
Unforgettable companions—Big Daddy and Doc
Matthews. These lively, boisterous characters infuse the
narrative with humor and heart, offering comic relief while
proving that even the darkest paths can be
Illuminated by friendship and camaraderie.
Together, they navigate a landscape fraught with danger
and deception, facing obstacles that test their resolve and
challenge their beliefs. This tale is not only about the
pursuit of a killer but also about finding strength in
vulnerability and forging unbreakable bonds along the
way.

As you delve into this captivating narrative, prepare to be entertained and moved, as it skillfully balances moments of tension with laughter and warmth. It is a story that reminds us that even in the face of tragedy, hope can rise anew, and redemption can be found in the most unexpected places.

So, saddle up and join this unlikely trio on a journey of justice, healing, and the enduring power of love. Welcome to a tale that is as rich in history as it is in heart—a wild ride through the rugged terrain of the human spirit.

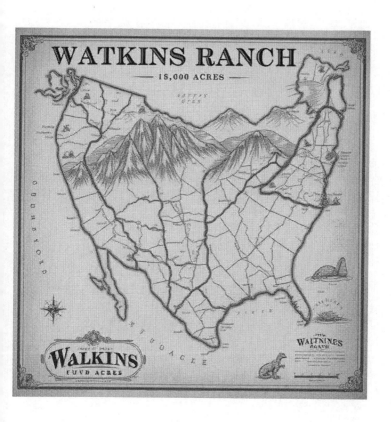

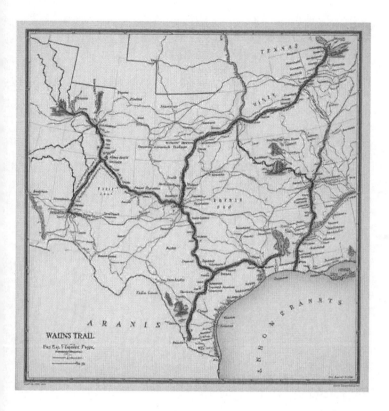

WAINS TRAIL

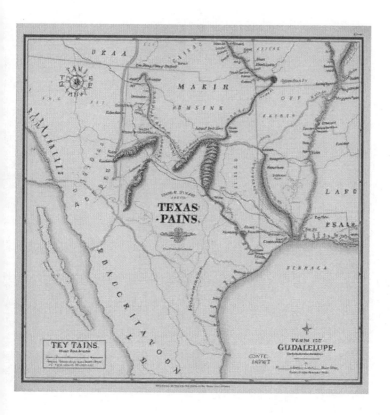

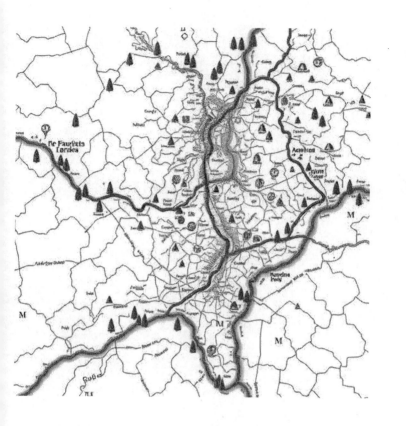

CHAPTER 1:
NEW BEGINNINGS

The spring of 1875 came late to Texas, arriving on the heels of one of the harshest winters anyone could remember. Cattle had died by the hundreds, crops had withered in their winter beds, and more than a few homesteads stood empty, their owners having packed up and headed back East in search of easier fortunes. But spring, when it finally arrived, painted the hills around Guadalupe Pass in colors that made even the most hardened soul believe in miracles. Bluebonnets carpeted the hills in swaths of purple-blue, Indian paintbrush dotted the valleys with splashes of crimson, and the morning glories that climbed my revival tent's poles opened their faces to the sun each dawn like faithful congregants at prayer.

I was twenty years old that spring, fresh from my training at the seminary in Little Rock, with nothing but my Bible, my wagon, and what I thought was an unshakeable certainty about my path in life. The Good Lord has a way of humbling even His most confident servants, though He usually does it with more gentleness than He showed me.

The town of Guadalupe Pass barely deserved the name in those days. A handful of wooden buildings clustered around a dusty main street, a general store that doubled as a post office, two saloons that did steady business, and a small white church that had stood empty since its previous minister had succumbed to typhoid fever the year before.

The townspeople had written to the Baptist Association in Arkansas, begging for someone to come lead a revival, to breathe life back into their spiritual community.

When the letter reached our seminary, I practically leaped at the chance.

"You're too young," Professor Matthews had warned me, his steel-gray eyebrows drawing together in concern. "These border towns need a steady hand, someone with experience. The war may be ten years past, but its shadows still lie heavy on these places."

But youth has a way of believing itself invincible, and I had argued my case with the passion of the truly convinced. "These people need hope," I'd insisted. "They need to be reminded of God's love and mercy. Who better to remind them than someone who still believes in both with his whole heart?"

The professor had studied me for a long moment, his weathered face unreadable.

Finally, he'd sighed and signed the authorization letter.

"Very well, Brother Wright. But remember this – preaching isn't just about knowing the Word. It's about knowing people's hearts."

My own father had expressed similar doubts when I'd announced my plans for a six-day revival. "Son," he'd said, his calloused hands resting heavy on my shoulders, "there's more kinds of hunger than what can be fed with scripture alone." I hadn't understood his meaning then. Sometimes I think back to that moment and wonder if he'd had some premonition of what lay ahead.

The preparations for the revival consumed my days. I'd arrived two weeks early to set up the tent and make arrangements, determined to do everything properly. The tent itself was a marvel – white canvas that glowed like an earthbound cloud when the sun hit it just right, with enough seating for two hundred souls. I'd borrowed it from the Association, promising to return it in better condition than I'd received it.

Every morning, I'd rise before dawn for prayer and meditation, then spend hours practicing my sermons.

I'd chosen my texts carefully – stories of redemption and new beginnings, of God's mercy triumphing over judgment. In the afternoons, I'd walk the town, introducing myself to shopkeepers and ranchers, extending personal invitations to the services. The saloon keepers eyed me with barely concealed amusement, but even they were polite enough, something I attributed to my height and broad shoulders rather than any respect for my collar.

Word spread quickly through the surrounding countryside that a revival was coming. Farmers and ranchers began making plans to attend, preparing wagons and setting aside evening chores. Even in those harsh times – or perhaps because of them – people hungered for something to believe in.

The first three days of the revival had gone well enough. Each evening, the tent filled with a mix of townspeople and country folk, all dressed in their Sunday best despite the dust that seemed to coat everything in this part of Texas. Women fanned themselves with church bulletins while children squirmed on hard wooden benches, and men sat with their hats in their laps, their faces carefully neutral as they sized up this young preacher from Arkansas.

I preached about Daniel in the lion's den, about David facing Goliath, about Moses leading his people to freedom – safe stories that I could tell with the confidence of youth and inexperience. The singing was enthusiastic, if not always on key, and each night a few more people would come forward during the altar call, seeking prayer or salvation or maybe just a moment of human connection.

Sarah, my oldest sister, had tried to prepare me for this work. "Remember," she'd written in her last letter, "people don't come to revival meetings just to hear about God. They come because they're hurting, because they're lonely, because they're looking for answers to questions they can't even put into words. Listen more than you preach, Victor. Sometimes that's the greatest ministry of all."

I thought I understood what she meant, but looking back now, I realize how naïve I was. I knew the words of faith, but I hadn't yet learned its heart. That lesson was about to come in a way I never could have expected.
It was on the fourth evening when everything changed. The service was already underway, the congregation swaying to "Amazing Grace," when she slipped in through the back of the tent like a shadow seeking shelter from the storm. Even with her face half-hidden by a worn calico bonnet, I could see the bruises she was trying to conceal.

My sermon that night was on redemption, though looking back, I was the one about to learn its true meaning.
The whispers reached my ears betwe"n verses – Michelle Kelly, they said, caught in the grip of the local drunk's cruelty. The women clucked their tongues in sympathy while the men looked away, unwilling to involve

themselves in what they saw as private business. My blood boiled at their indifference, but I kept preaching, though I found my eyes drawn to her repeatedly throughout the service.

She sat perfectly still in the back row, her hands folded in her lap, but there was something about her presence that commanded attention. Perhaps it was the way she held herself, straight-backed and proud despite her obvious injuries, or maybe it was the intensity with which she listened to every word. When I spoke about God's love for the broken-hearted, I saw her fingers clench tightly around her worn Bible.

Later, I would learn that she had come to the revival that night fully intending to end her life afterward. She'd already written letters to her mother and brothers, already chosen the spot down by the river where they would find her. But something in the words I preached – or perhaps something in the God who had led her there – caught hold of her heart and wouldn't let go.

The revival grew more Intense over the next two days, but Michelle Kelly remained in her back-row seat, neither coming forward nor slipping away early. She simply watched, listened, and waited. I noticed she came earlier each night, though always alone, and always wearing long sleeves despite the Texas heat. The bruises on her face were fading to yellow, but new ones had appeared on her wrists – dark purple bands that made my hands clench into fists when I glimpsed them.

On that final night, after I'd given the last benediction of the revival, I lingered longer than usual, packing up my belongings for the long journey back to Arkansas. The moon was high and full, casting sharp shadows across the deserted revival grounds. The last of the townsfolk had long since returned to their homes, leaving only the sound of crickets and the distant howl of a coyote.

I was loading the last of the hymnals into my wagon when she appeared beside me, silent as a ghost. Up close, I could see she was younger than I'd thought, probably no more than eighteen or nineteen. Fresh blood trickled from her split lip, and her right eye was swelling shut.
"I'm sorry to trouble you, Reverend," she said, her voice barely above a whisper. "I just… I didn't know where else to turn."

The sight of her injuries in the moonlight stirred something fierce in my chest – not just anger at whoever had hurt her, but a deeper emotion I couldn't quite name. I led her to sit on the wagon's tailgate and soaked my handkerchief in water from my canteen. As I gently cleaned her wounds, she began to talk, the words pouring out like a dam had broken.

"He wasn't always like this," she said softly, wincing as I dabbed at her lip. "When we first married, he was so kind. Brought me flowers every Sunday, read to me from his mother's poetry books. I thought I was the luckiest girl in Texas." She gave a bitter laugh that turned into a sob. "Mama tried to warn me. Said she saw something in his eyes that weren't right, but I wouldn't listen. Thought I knew better than everyone else."

We talked through the night, watching the stars wheel overhead while she shared her story. Her father had been a cattle rancher, a good man who'd taught her to ride and shoot before she was ten years old. He'd died when she was twelve, trampled by a spooked horse during a spring roundup. After that, her mother had somehow managed to keep their small ranch running, raising three children on nothing but grit and grace.

"Mama could do anything," Michelle said, her voice taking on a warmth I hadn't heard before. "She'd be up before dawn making biscuits, then out mending fences until sundown. Never complained, never asked for help. Just did what needed doing."

They'd managed well enough until the drought of '67 took most of their herd.

After that, it had been a slow slide into poverty, with Michelle eventually marrying the first man who offered what seemed like security. That security had turned out to be a prison of fists and cruel words.

"First time he hit me, he cried afterward," she said, staring out into the darkness. "Got down on his knees and begged my forgiveness, swore it would never happen again.

Said it was the whiskey that made him do it, that he'd stop drinking." She touched her swollen eye gently. "But the whiskey didn't stop, and neither did he."

As she spoke, I found myself studying her profile in the moonlight. Despite everything she'd endured, there was a strength in her features that spoke of deep resilience.

Her hands, though small, were callused from hard work. She held herself with a dignity that all the bruises in the world couldn't diminish.

When dawn began to paint the sky in shades of pink and gold, she stood to leave, straightening her threadbare shawl with as much dignity as a queen adjusting her ermine. "I appreciate your kindness," she said, her voice stronger than it had been hours before.

"I just wish…" She didn't finish the thought, but I heard it clear as Sunday bells: I wish I didn't have to go back. Maybe it was the Spirit moving, or maybe just the foolishness of youth, but before I could catch my tongue, I said, "Well, you don't have to go back."

The look she gave me could have stopped a charging bull. "Oh yeah?" she said with a bitter laugh that held no humor. "And where exactly am I supposed to go?"

"With me."

I've never seen anyone's eyes go quite that wide. She took a step back, studying me like I'd just sprouted wings and a halo. The rising sun caught the gold flecks in her brown eyes, making them seem to spark with an inner fire. "Just what kind of woman do you take me for, Reverend?" Her hand strayed to the pocket of her dress, and I remembered the rumors about her skill with a knife.

"A woman who deserves better than what life's given her so far," I replied honestly. "Look, I've got a sister in Arkansas – Sarah. She's got a big house and four little ones she's raising on her own since her husband passed. She's always saying how she needs help, and you'd have a safe place to stay while you figure out what you want to do next."

I could see the war being waged behind her eyes – hope fighting with suspicion, desperation wrestling with pride. "And what do you get out of this arrangement?" she asked, her voice sharp with distrust.

"The satisfaction of knowing I didn't leave someone in danger when I could have helped," I replied, meeting her gaze steadily. "Nothing more."

She studied me for what felt like hours, though it couldn't have been more than a minute. I could see her weighing every possibility, searching my face for any sign of deception. Finally, she squared her shoulders and said, "Fine," jumping up onto the wagon seat like she'd been doing it all her life.

"But if you try anything improper, Reverend, I should warn you – I'm a fair hand with a knife."

I couldn't help but laugh at that. "Ma'am, I assure you, my intentions are purely charitable. Besides," I added, climbing up beside her, "my mama would rise from her grave and tan my hide if I did anything to dishonor a lady." The sun was fully up now, painting the world in shades of gold and promise.

As I clicked my tongue to set the horses in motion, I sent up a silent prayer of thanks – and maybe a small request for guidance. I had no idea what I was getting myself into, but something in my soul told me this was exactly where I was meant to be.

As we headed east, leaving Guadalupe Pass behind us, I discovered Michelle Kelly was quite the talker once she felt safe. The miles rolled by under our wagon wheels as she told me about her life before everything went wrong. Her voice grew animated as she shared stories of her childhood, and I found myself enchanted by the way she told them, her hands dancing in the air as she spoke.

"You should have seen Mama when she was breaking horses," she said, laughing at the memory. "She'd put on Pa's old britches under her skirt – scandalous, I know – and she could gentle the wildest mustang you ever saw. Used to say there wasn't a horse born that couldn't be won over with patience and respect." Her smile faded slightly. "Guess that wisdom doesn't apply so well to people."

The morning sun warmed our faces as we traveled, and a gentle breeze carried the scent of wildflowers. I pointed out a red-tailed hawk circling overhead, but Michelle had spotted it long before I did. She knew the names of plants I'd never noticed before, could read the weather in the way the wind shifted, and had an uncanny sense of when we needed to rest the horses.

"My pa taught me all about trail riding before he passed," she explained as we stopped to water the horses at a small creek. "Said a woman ought to know how to take care of herself out here." She patted one of the horses' necks. "These are good animals. Strong legs, good confirmation. You chose well."
"My brother helped me pick them," I admitted. "Truth be told, I know more about scripture than horseflesh."

She laughed at that, a real laugh this time, not the bitter sound I'd heard earlier.

"Well, Reverend Wright, looks like we might be able to help each other then. You can teach me about the Good Book, and I'll teach you about horses."

It was only then that I realized I hadn't properly introduced myself. "Victor," I said, feeling oddly shy. "My name's Victor."

"Victor," she repeated, testing the name. "It suits you. Better than 'Reverend' anyway. You're awful young to be carrying such a serious title."

Around midday, we stopped to eat some of the provisions the church ladies had packed for my journey home. As we sat in the shade of a live oak tree, sharing cornbread and cold chicken, I found myself studying her when she wasn't looking. The bruises on her face couldn't hide her natural beauty, but it was more than that. There was a quiet strength about her, a resilience that showed in the way she held herself.

"Tell me about your family," she said suddenly. "What kind of folks raised a boy to become a preacher so young?"

I told her about my father, a carpenter who could build anything from a cradle to a church steeple, and my mother, who'd taught all seven of us children to read using the Bible and Shakespeare's sonnets. I told her about my four sisters – Sarah, the oldest, who we'd be staying with; Mary, who could outcook anyone in three counties; Ruth, who was studying to be a teacher; and Rachel, the youngest, who was more comfortable on a horse than in a parlor.

"And two brothers," I added. "James works with Pa in the carpentry business, and John's studying law in Little Rock. Though if you ask Ma, she'll tell you she's got eight children – she counts Jesus as her firstborn."

That made Michelle smile. "Your mama sounds like quite a woman."

"She was," I said softly. "We lost her to fever two winters ago."

Michelle reached over and touched my hand briefly. "I'm sorry. It's not easy losing a parent." The simple gesture of comfort sent a warmth through me that had nothing to do with the Texas sun.

As evening approached, we looked for a place to make camp. Michelle spotted a perfect site – a sheltered area near a creek, with good grass for the horses and plenty of dry wood for a fire.

While I set up the tent, she gathered firewood, but when she returned, she fixed me with a suspicious look that stopped me in my tracks.

"I see you're only setting up one tent," she said bluntly. "I know you ain't expecting me to share it with you. Or did you have other plans in mind?"

I felt my face flame red hot. Truth was, at twenty years old, my experience with women was limited to one fumbled encounter with a neighbor girl when I was thirteen – an incident that earned me the worst whipping of my life from my father. "Ma'am," I said, drawing myself up as dignified as I could manage, "if I had any such intentions, I wouldn't have waited until we were out here in the middle of nowhere.

The tent is yours. I'll sleep in the wagon."

She turned about five shades of red herself, then hurried off to fetch supplies for supper, muttering something under her breath that I couldn't quite catch. When she returned, she had a grin I'd never seen before on any woman's face – part amusement, part appreciation, and something else that made my heart skip a beat.

That night, she cooked up a supper that would have made my mama proud. The beans were seasoned perfect, the taters crispy on the outside and soft within, and the cornbread was so light it practically floated off the plate. She moved around the campfire with a grace that seemed at odds with her earlier wariness, humming hymns under her breath as she worked.

The firelight caught in her hair, turning the brown strands to copper and gold, and I found myself mesmerized by the way she seemed to dance rather than walk. There was something about her that made me want to build a future, plant roots, create a home. But I kept these thoughts to myself, knowing she needed time to heal, to find her own strength again.

As we sat by the fire after supper, Michelle asked about the sister we'd be staying with. "Tell me about Sarah," she said. "What kind of woman is she?"

"The best kind," I replied without hesitation. "She lost her husband in a logging accident two years ago, but she hasn't let it break her. Keeps her farm running, raises her children, and still finds time to help anyone in need. She's got a way of making everyone feel like family."

"And you're sure she won't mind taking in a stranger?"
"Sarah's got the biggest heart in Arkansas," I assured her. "She's always saying the
Good Lord never meant for anyone to face their troubles alone."
Michelle was quiet for a long moment, staring into the flames. "I've never had anyone just… help before.

Not without wanting something in return."
"Well, get used to it," I said, trying to keep my voice light despite the anger her words stirred in my heart. "Where we're heading, helping folks is just what we do."
As the stars wheeled overhead that first night, with the fire burning low and the crickets singing their evening chorus, I felt a peace I hadn't known in years.

The evening wrapped around us like a comfortable blanket, and our conversation flowed as naturally as the creek beside our camp. Michelle had a way of making silence feel comfortable, something I'd never mastered despite all my preaching.

"Can I ask you something personal?" she said after a while, adding another small log to the fire. When I nodded, she continued, "Why did you really become a preacher? You're so young… there must have been other things you wanted to do."

The question made me pause. No one had asked me that before – not even my family. They'd all just assumed it was a natural calling, given how much time I'd spent in church growing up. But Michelle's direct gaze demanded honesty. "I was sixteen when I first felt the call," I said slowly, choosing my words carefully. "It was during the yellow fever outbreak of '71. People were dying all around us, and the local preacher – Reverend Johnson – he just…

he never stopped. Day and night, he was there for everyone, bringing comfort, food, medicine. Didn't matter if they were Baptist, Methodist, or hadn't seen the inside of a church in years. He showed me that being a minister isn't just about preaching on Sundays. It's about being Christ's hands and feet in a broken world."

I paused, remembering those dark days. "Reverend Johnson died that summer, caught the fever himself. But before he passed, he told me something I'll never forget. He said, 'Son, God doesn't call the qualified. He qualifies the called.' Two weeks later, I preached my first sermon." Michelle considered this, her face thoughtful in the firelight. "And you've never regretted it? Never wished for a simpler life?"

"There are days," I admitted, "when I wonder if I'm doing any good at all. Days when the burden feels too heavy. But then something happens – someone finds hope, or healing, or just a moment of peace – and I know this is exactly where I'm supposed to be."

She nodded, understanding in her eyes. "Like tonight? Helping a strange woman run away from her husband?" "You're not running away," I corrected gently. "You're running toward something better. There's a difference."

The night grew cooler, and Michelle pulled her shawl tighter around her shoulders.

Without thinking, I shrugged off my coat and offered it to her. She hesitated for just a moment before accepting it, wrapping herself in the worn wool.

"Tell me more about Arkansas," she said, her voice growing sleepy. "What's it really like there?"

I painted her a picture of my home – the rolling hills covered in pine and oak, the clear streams full of fish, the wild blackberries that grew thick along the fencerows in summer. I told her about the little town near Sarah's farm, about the general store where old men played checkers on the front porch, about the one-room schoolhouse where children learned their letters and numbers.

"It sounds like paradise," she murmured.

"It's not perfect," I said honestly. "We have our share of troubles. But it's a good place to heal. To start over."

The fire had burned down to embers when Michelle finally stood to retire to the tent. She started to hand back my coat, but I told her to keep it for the night. As she turned to go, she paused.

"Victor?" Her voice was soft, uncertain. "Thank you. Not just for helping me, but for… for seeing me. Really seeing me."

Before I could respond, she disappeared into the tent, leaving me with a strange ache in my chest that had nothing to do with physical hunger. I settled into the wagon for the night, using my saddle as a pillow, and stared up at the star-filled sky. My seminary professors would probably have plenty to say about the impropriety of traveling alone with a young woman, even with the purest of intentions. But as I lay there, listening to the night sounds of the Texas prairie, I couldn't bring myself to care about propriety.

I thought about what my father had said about different kinds of hunger, and finally understood his meaning. Michelle wasn't just hungry for safety or security – she was starving for basic human dignity, for someone to see her worth beyond her circumstances. And maybe, in trying to help her find those things, I was satisfying a hunger in my own soul that I hadn't even recognized.

Sleep was slow in coming that night. My mind kept drifting to the way she'd looked in the firelight, to the sound of her laugh when it was real and unguarded, to the strength that showed through her brokenness. I tried to tell myself it was foolish to feel this way about a woman I'd just met, especially one who'd suffered such trauma.

But there was something about Michelle that made me want to build a future, plant roots, create a home. I heard her stirring in the tent, probably finding it as hard to sleep as I was. After a while, her voice drifted out, soft and clear, singing an old hymn I remembered from my childhood: "Amazing grace, how sweet the sound, that saved a wretch like me…" The words floated on the night air, a promise of redemption and new beginnings.

Little did I know then that this journey was just the beginning of our story, and that the trials ahead would test every bit of faith and love we were building around that first campfire.

The Lord works in mysterious ways, they say, and His plan for us was more mysterious – and more wonderful – than anything I could have imagined that spring evening in Texas.

As dawn broke the next morning, I woke to find Michelle already up, stoking the remains of last night's fire to make coffee. She'd washed her face in the creek, and in the early morning light, I could see past the bruises to the woman she must have been before – the woman she could be again. She caught me watching her and smiled, a real smile that reached her eyes.

"Ready to face another day, Reverend?" she asked, pouring coffee into a tin cup and holding it out to me.

"With you by my side? Always," I replied without thinking, then felt my face grow hot at my own boldness.

But Michelle just laughed, a sound as fresh and promising as the morning itself. "Well then," she said, "let's see what the Good Lord has in store for us today."

And so began our journey together, two broken souls finding healing in each other's company, guided by a faith that was bigger than our fears and a hope that outweighed our doubts. The road ahead was long and would prove more dangerous than either of us could have imagined, but in that moment, watching the sun rise over the Texas hills with Michelle beside me, I knew with absolute certainty that this was exactly where God meant me to be.

CHAPTER 2:
NEEDLE IN A HAYSTACK

Hope is a peculiar thing. It can make a man forget about the dangers that lurk behind him, about the consequences that trail like shadows on a westward path. That second morning on the trail, watching Michelle sip her coffee in the dawn light, I let myself believe we'd made a clean escape. The morning had dawned clear and cool, with just enough bite in the air to make the coffee steam rise like prayer into the purple-gray sky.

We'd slept well despite our unusual arrangements — me in the wagon, her in the tent — and the new day seemed full of promise.
I remember every detail of those last peaceful moments, the way you remember the calm before a storm breaks. Michelle had washed her face in the creek, and the morning light softened the bruises that marked her skin.

Her hair was tied back with a faded blue ribbon she'd found in her pocket, and she'd borrowed one of my clean shirts to replace her torn one. It hung loose on her smaller frame, but somehow that only made her look more alive, more herself, as if she were slowly shedding the shell of her old life.

"You know," she said, passing me a tin cup of coffee, "I've been thinking about your sister's farm. Do you think she might let me help with the children? I always wanted to teach, before…" She let the sentence trail off, but I understood. Before James. Before the dreams got beaten out of her.

"Sarah would love that," I replied, watching the sunrise paint color into the Texas landscape. "Her oldest, Mary Beth, is already reading at a high level. She's got her mama's quick mind."

Michelle smiled, and for a moment, I saw the woman she must have been before – young, hopeful, full of dreams. "It's strange," she said softly, "but for the first time in years, I'm actually looking forward to tomorrow."

That's when we heard the first riders approaching.

I didn't recognize the danger at first. Out here, the sound of approaching horses could mean anything – rangers on patrol, cowboys moving cattle, travelers on the trail. But Michelle – Michelle knew. I watched the hope drain from her face like water through sand, replaced by a terror so deep it made my heart stop.

"Victor." Her voice was barely a whisper, the coffee cup trembling in her hands. "That's Thunder's walk – I'd know it anywhere. James's stallion, the one he bought just to prove he could outspend my father's ghost. And he's not alone."

She was right. As I listened more carefully, I could distinguish at least four different horses approaching, their hoofbeats echoing off the low hills that surrounded our camp.

We had maybe two minutes before they'd be in sight. "How?" I asked, already moving to gather our essential supplies. "How did they find us so quickly?"

Michelle's laugh was bitter as she helped me pack. "In a town like Guadalupe Pass? Probably didn't take more than one person seeing which way we headed. James has friends everywhere – or at least, people who owe him money or favors. And the Carson brothers…" She shuddered. "They can track a fox through a flood."

"The Carson brothers?" The name sent a chill down my spine. During my time in Guadalupe Pass, I'd heard plenty about the Carsons. They'd started as cattle rustlers, graduated to hired guns, and now they operated in that gray space between lawman and outlaw, doing whatever dirty work paid the most. The fact that James had brought them along told me everything I needed to know about his intentions.

I had about thirty seconds to make a decision that would change both our lives forever. We could stand our ground – after all, we'd done nothing legally wrong. No law prevented a married woman from traveling, and as a minister, my reputation might offer some protection. Or we could run, betraying our guilt but buying precious time to get further away from Guadalupe Pass and James's sphere of influence.

Looking at Michelle's face, seeing the terror there alongside a fierce determination not to go back, I made my choice.
"Get in the wagon," I said quietly, already reaching for the reins. "And Michelle?
Whatever happens next, remember – God didn't bring us this far to abandon us now."

She nodded once, sharply, then began moving with the efficient grace I'd noticed yesterday. Within seconds, she had our essential supplies stowed and was climbing into the wagon. I couldn't help but admire her composure – this was a woman who knew how to handle a crisis. The thunder of approaching hooves grew louder as Michelle settled herself behind the wagon seat. I sent up a quick prayer, clicked my tongue at the horses, and set us on a course that would either deliver us to freedom or lead us straight into disaster.

"They'll try to cut us off at Miller's Creek," Michelle said, her voice steady despite her fear. "It's the only good crossing for miles. But there's another way, if you trust me."

"I trust you," I replied without hesitation, and I meant it. In the short time I'd known her, Michelle had shown more courage and character than most people I'd known my whole life.

She leaned forward, pointing to a line of trees in the distance. "Head for that cottonwood grove. There's a buffalo trail through there that leads to a different crossing. Pa used it during the war, when Confederate patrols were watching the main roads."

The canvas cover of our wagon snapped in the wind as we picked up speed, the sound like gunshots in the tense morning air.

I'd never pushed horses this hard this early, but fear has a way of making you forget about conventional wisdom. The wagon rattled and creaked, protesting the pace and the rough ground.

Behind us, the riders crested the hill we'd just descended. Michelle knelt up to look back, and I felt her tense.

"Four of them," she reported, her voice clipped. "James is leading – he's the one on Thunder. Cole Matthews is with him – he manages the saloon, does whatever James asks, no matter how dirty. And both Carson brothers." She spat the name like it tasted bad. "Luke and Matthew Carson. They're twins, mean as snakes and twice as deadly.

They won't care that you're a preacher – might even see that as a reason to be crueler."

I'd heard stories about the Carsons during my time in Guadalupe Pass, whispered tales in the general store and around evening fires. They hadn't always been bad men, folks said. Their father had been a respected rancher until Yankees burned him out during the war. The boys had watched him die, then spent the rest of the war riding with Quantrill's Raiders, learning the worst kinds of violence.

Now they hired out to whoever paid the most, and they had a particular hatred for anyone who represented law or morality.

The wagon hit a rough patch of ground, and I heard something crack ominously beneath us. The horses were already lathered, their hooves throwing up clumps of earth as they ran. Behind us, the riders were gaining ground, their fresher horses eating up the distance between us. The first shot came without warning, the bullet whistling past close enough that I felt the air move against my ear. Michelle ducked instinctively but then straightened up, her face set with a determination that transformed her.

Gone was the frightened woman from the revival tent – in her place sat a rancher's daughter who knew how to fight. She reached into the back of the wagon and came up with my old Springfield rifle. I'd bought it after the war for five dollars and a promise to pray for the seller's soul. It wasn't much to look at, but it was accurate and reliable – much like its current holder.

"I thought ministers weren't supposed to carry guns," she said, checking to see if it was loaded. Her hands moved over the weapon with practiced familiarity.

"We're also supposed to turn the other cheek," I replied, steering around a fallen log that could have broken our axle. "But sometimes the Good Lord expects us to use the sense He gave us. My daddy always said Jesus never meant for us to let evil men do as they please."

Another shot rang out, this one splintering the wooden seat between us. Splinters flew, and I felt a sharp sting as one caught my cheek. Michelle muttered something that definitely wasn't a prayer and turned, bracing the rifle against the wagon seat. The crack of her shot echoed across the prairie, followed by a cry of surprise and pain. "Did you…?" I couldn't finish the question.

"Just winged Cole's horse," she said, already reloading with steady hands. "Pa taught me to shoot better than that, but a moving wagon makes it tricky." There was a fierce light in her eyes I hadn't seen before. "He always said, 'Aim to warn first, kill if you must, but never shoot without being ready to face the consequences before God.'"

The memory of her father seemed to strengthen her, and I saw then what she must have been like before James broke her spirit – proud, capable, full of life. The woman beside me wasn't running from something; she was running toward the person she was meant to be.

Thunder's distinctive hoofbeats were getting closer. The big stallion lived up to his name, each strike of his hooves against the earth like a hammer blow. James's voice carried on the wind, thick with rage and whiskey.

"Michelle!" he bellowed. "You stop this foolishness right now, woman! Ain't nowhere in Texas you can hide from me!"

I felt her stiffen beside me, but when she spoke, her voice rang with conviction. "Better dead in a ditch than back with you, James Kelly! You don't own me anymore!"

The creek came into view, a line of cottonwoods marking its course through the prairie. The trees were just beginning to leaf out, their pale green buds a promise of spring renewal that seemed at odds with our desperate flight. But our horses were failing, their stride shortening as exhaustion set in.

The pursuing riders were close enough now that I could hear the Carsons laughing, enjoying the chase like wolves running down prey.

We hit the creek crossing hard, water spraying up as the wheels crashed through. The wagon lurched sickeningly, and I heard another crack from somewhere underneath. The sound reminded me of the way Mama's china had shattered when the fever took her – a sharp, final sort of breaking.

"We're not going to make it much further," I said, fighting to keep the horses on track. "The wagon's about done for."

Michelle pointed to a cut bank partially hidden by brush. "There! Behind those willows – there's a trail up to the cave. Pa used it during the war, when raiders were about. Said it was his ace in the hole."

I turned the wagon sharply, the wheels skidding in the mud. Behind us, I heard shouts of triumph as our pursuers thought they had us cornered.

They didn't know these lands like Michelle did, didn't understand that sometimes the best hiding place is the one right under your nose.

The trail was barely wide enough for the wagon, and steep enough that the horses struggled for every step. Branches whipped at our faces as we climbed. The wheels hit rocks and roots, each impact sending shudders through the failing structure.

Just when I thought we couldn't go any further, Michelle touched my arm.

"Stop here," she whispered. "The cave's just ahead, but we need to unhitch the horses first. And…" she hesitated, "Victor, if anything happens to me, you need to know something. In the cave, there's a letter my pa wrote before he died. It proves James isn't who he claims to be. It's hidden behind the third barrel on the left side. Promise me you'll find it."

"Nothing's going to happen to you," I said firmly, but I memorized the location anyway. "We're in this together, remember?"

Working quickly and quietly, we managed to free the horses from their harness. The poor beasts were trembling with exhaustion, their sides heaving. Michelle led them through a narrow gap in the rocks, whispering soothingly to them in that way horse-people have.

The cave entrance was well-hidden, exactly the kind of place a smart rancher would use to store supplies – or to hide from enemies during troubled times.

We'd barely gotten the horses inside when we heard the riders below, their voices echoing off the creek bank. I recognized James's voice first, slurred with drink but sharp with malice.

"Spread out!" he commanded. "Luke, you and Matthew take the high ground. Cole, check downstream. That wagon couldn't have disappeared into thin air."

"They must've gone upstream," Luke Carson's voice drifted up. "No way they could climb this bluff with a wagon."

"Shut your mouth and keep looking," James snarled.

"I want that preacher's head on a pike, and I want my wife back where she belongs. No man steals from James Kelly and lives to brag about it."

Michelle and I stood in the darkness of the cave, barely breathing, as the sounds of the search continued below. She was trembling, but when I reached for her hand, her grip was strong.

Through our joined hands, I could feel her pulse racing, but her breathing was steady. This was a woman who knew how to face fear.

We stayed that way for what seemed like hours, listening as the voices gradually faded into the distance. The cave was cool and damp, smelling of limestone and earth.

Somewhere in its depths, water dripped with a steady rhythm that reminded me of church bells marking time. Finally, when the only sounds were the horses' quiet breathing and that steady drip, Michelle let out a shaky laugh.

"Well, Reverend," she said, "I hope you're ready for a long day of hiding, because they won't give up easy. James Kelly never could stand to lose anything he thought belonged to him."

I squeezed her hand gently. "I meant what I said before – God didn't bring us this far to abandon us now."

"Maybe not," she replied, her voice thoughtful in the darkness. "But He might be testing just how much faith we really have."

As if in answer, we heard a distant shout, followed by the sound of hooves returning. Our test of faith, it seemed, was just beginning.

The cave opened before us like a church after dark, vast and reverent in its silence. As our eyes adjusted to the darkness, I could make out the careful organization of supplies along the walls – evidence of a man who believed in preparing for the worst while praying for the best. Michelle moved through the space with familiar ease, her fingers trailing along the rough limestone walls as if greeting an old friend.

"Pa started storing supplies here during the war," she whispered, leading us deeper into the cave. "Said a man needed three things to survive: a good horse, a hidden cache, and faith in the Almighty. Sometimes I think he knew something like this would happen."

Her voice caught slightly. "He never did trust James." She found a lantern among the supplies but didn't light it immediately. Instead, she guided us and the horses further back, where the cave widened into a natural chamber. The air was cool and damp, carrying the mineral scent of underground water and the earthier smell of the horses. Somewhere in the darkness, water dripped with metronome precision.

"The chamber branches here," Michelle explained softly. "One tunnel leads to a spring – that's where the dripping comes from. The other goes back about fifty feet to what Pa called the sleeping room. He set it up during the war, when raiders were thick in these parts."

As we settled the horses in a wider section of the cave, I couldn't help but admire the forethought that had gone into this hiding place. There were feeding troughs carved into the rock, old blankets for bedding, even some musty hay that the horses immediately began investigating.

Once we were deep enough in the cave, Michelle finally lit the lantern, keeping the flame low. In its dim light, I could see the strain of the morning's events written on her face. The bruises from her last encounter with James stood out starkly against her pale skin, but there was a new strength in her bearing – as if each mile we put between her and Guadalupe Pass helped her reclaim a piece of herself. "You're quite the shot," I said, trying to distract her from dark thoughts. "I don't recall that being mentioned in the revival meetings."

She smiled faintly, setting the lantern on a natural shelf in the rock. "Didn't seem proper to brag about my shooting skills in church. Besides," her smile faded, "James didn't like me talking about anything from before. Said it wasn't fitting for his wife to know more about guns and horses than he did."

"Tell me about before," I said gently. "Tell me about your father."

Michelle was quiet for a long moment, and I worried I'd overstepped. But then she began to speak, her voice soft but clear in the cave's darkness.

"Pa was different from most men around here. He believed in education – had books shipped all the way from New Orleans. Said a person needed to feed their mind same as their body." She smiled at the memory. "He taught me to shoot and ride, sure, but he also taught me Shakespeare and geometry. Said a woman ought to be able to calculate the area of a field and quote sonnets while she's plowing it."

A shout from outside made us both freeze. The voices were closer now, and I could make out fragments of conversation echoing off the cliff face.
"...tracks end here..."

"...check the high ground..."
"...can't have gone far..."
Michelle's grip on my hand tightened. We sat in tense silence as footsteps crunched on the rocks above our hiding place. Dust and small pebbles rained down through cracks in the cave ceiling. I found myself praying harder than I ever had during any revival service.

The footsteps paused directly overhead. "Hey James!" Luke Carson's voice carried clearly through the rock. "You sure they came this way? Ain't nothing up here but rocks and rattlers."

James's response was thick with fury and whiskey. "Keep looking! They're around here somewhere. That preacher's got my property, and I aim to get it back."
I felt Michelle stiffen beside me. "Property," she whispered, her voice trembling with anger rather than fear. "That's all I ever was to him.

Property to own, property to beat, property to break." She pulled away from me, moving toward the barrels her father had stored. "It's time you knew the truth about James Kelly."

She counted three barrels in from the left, then reached behind them, feeling along the rock wall. After a moment, she withdrew a leather packet, its surface dark with age. "Pa wrote this the day before he died," she said, returning to sit beside me. "I found it two months ago, hidden in his Bible.

That's when everything changed – when James caught me reading it."

She opened the packet carefully, drawing out several sheets of paper covered in faded but neat handwriting. In the lantern's dim light, I could see that they were shaking slightly in her hands.

"My father wasn't killed by a spooked horse," she said quietly. "He was murdered. And James Kelly isn't really James Kelly at all."

In the flickering lantern light, Michelle's hands steadied as she unfolded her father's letter. Above us, footsteps continued to move back and forth, but we were both focused on the pages before us. Her father's handwriting was clear and strong, like the man himself had been.

"My dearest Michelle," she read softly, "If you're reading this, then my fears were justified, and I didn't live long enough to protect you from what's coming. The man who calls himself James Kelly is really James Thaddeus Morton, wanted in three states for murder and worse crimes. I discovered his true identity two days ago, when an old friend from the Rangers passed through..."

Michelle's voice caught, and I gently took the letter from her trembling hands.

Picking up where she left off, I read:

"Morton rode with Quantrill's Raiders during the war, but not as a soldier – as a spy and murderer. He would gain people's trust, learn their secrets, then betray them to the raiders. After the war, he took up with a gang that preyed on struggling ranches, using the same tactics.

He courts daughters of property owners, marries them, then arranges 'accidents' for their fathers. Once he has control of the property through his wife, he sells everything off and disappears, leaving devastation in his wake.

I've gathered proof of his true identity, including witness statements and a wanted poster from Missouri. They're hidden in the strong box beneath the floorboards of my study. But if you're reading this, daughter, it means he got to me before I could expose him.

Michelle, my brave girl, you must be careful. Morton is more dangerous than any man
I've ever known. He has powerful friends and no conscience to stay his hand. If
anything happens to me, take these papers to Judge Richardson in Austin. He's an old friend and will know what to do.

Know that I love you with all my heart, and I'm sorry I couldn't protect you better. Trust in God, trust your instincts, and remember – you are stronger than you know. Your loving father,
Thomas Kelly"
The cave fell silent as I finished reading, save for the steady drip of water and the occasional shuffle of the horses. Michelle sat perfectly still, her face a mask of complex emotions.

"I found the strongbox," she said finally, her voice barely above a whisper. "But I was too late. James – Morton – had already emptied it. When he caught me searching the study..." She touched her face unconsciously, where the oldest bruises were just beginning to fade. "That's when the beatings got worse. He knew I was suspicious, knew I might expose him."

"Why didn't you run then?" I asked gently.
"He threatened to burn down the orphanage in town if I tried to leave. Said he'd make sure everyone knew it was my fault." She laughed bitterly. "He knows exactly how to control people. Knows their weaknesses, their fears. But when I saw you at the revival, preaching about God's deliverance..." She turned to me, her eyes bright in the lantern light. "Something changed. I felt hope for the first time in so long."

A sudden crash from above made us both jump. Voices filtered down through the rock:
"Found their wagon!" That was Cole Matthews. "All smashed up in the brush. They can't be far!"
"Search every cave and crevice!" James's voice was closer now, almost directly overhead. "And remember – I want the preacher alive. I aim to make an example of him."

Michelle quickly gathered the letters, securing them inside her dress. "We need to be ready to move," she whispered. "Once it gets dark..."
"You're not going anywhere."

The new voice came from the cave entrance, accompanied by the unmistakable sound of a hammer being cocked. Luke Carson stepped into the dim light of our lantern, his gun trained steadily on us.

Behind him, his brother Matthew emerged from the shadows, carrying a coil of rope.

"Well, well," Luke drawled, a cruel smile playing across his face. "Looks like the love birds found themselves a nice little nest. James!" he called out, his voice echoing through the cave. "We found your property!"

I started to move in front of Michelle, but she was faster. In one fluid motion, she grabbed the lantern and hurled it at Luke's face. The cave plunged into darkness as the lantern shattered, and all hell broke loose.

The sound of the gunshot was deafening in the enclosed space. I felt Michelle grab my hand, pulling me deeper into the cave. "The back tunnel!" she hissed. "Move!"

Behind us, curses and confusion erupted as the Carson brothers struggled in the darkness. The horses, spooked by the gunshot, added to the chaos with their frightened movements. More voices were approaching from the cave entrance – James and Cole, drawn by the commotion.

We ran blindly through the darkness, Michelle's knowledge of the cave our only guide.

The tunnel narrowed, forcing us to crouch and feel our way along the rough walls. Water dripped down our necks, and the air grew thinner. Behind us, lantern light began to fill the main chamber, accompanied by James's enraged shouting.

"Don't let them get away! There's no way out back there – it's a dead end!"

Michelle's grip on my hand tightened. "He's wrong," she whispered. "Pa showed me something... if we can just reach it..."

The tunnel grew narrower as we pressed forward, the rough limestone walls scraping our shoulders. The air was thick with mineral dust and the musty scent of age-old darkness. Behind us, lantern light flickered eerily against the cave walls, accompanied by the sound of pursuit. James's voice echoed through the passages, distorted by the rock until it sounded inhuman.

"You're only making it worse for yourself, Michelle! There's nowhere to go – this tunnel dead-ends in a hundred feet. You know what happens to people who cross me!"

"Almost there," Michelle whispered, tugging me forward. "Pa said to count the crystal formations on the left wall. One... two... three..." Her free hand traced along the rock face as we moved. "There should be a crack, wide enough for a person, just past the seventh formation."

The pursuing footsteps grew closer. A bullet struck the wall near my head, sending stone chips flying. The confined space made the gunshot sound like thunder, leaving my ears ringing. The horses we'd left behind whinnied in terror at the noise.

"Found the crack!" Michelle's voice was triumphant in the darkness. "Here – feel along this edge. Pa said it opens into an old water channel. The Comanche used it during raids, before the war."

I felt the opening with my hands — barely wide enough for shoulders if you turned sideways. Cold air breathed from it, carrying the promise of open space beyond. Behind us, the lantern light grew brighter.

"Ladies first," I whispered, helping Michelle position herself at the crack.

"Don't you dare try to be noble," she hissed back. "We go together or not at all."

Before I could argue, another shot rang out. This one found its mark — I felt a searing pain along my left arm as the bullet grazed me. Michelle's hands were instantly there, pulling me toward the crack.

"Move!" she ordered, all trace of fear gone from her voice. This was the woman her father had raised — decisive, strong, unafraid.

We squeezed through the opening together, the rough rock tearing at our clothes. The passage beyond was pitch black but larger, allowing us to stand upright. Water trickled somewhere ahead, its sound masking our footsteps.

"You can't hide forever!" James's voice was closer now, almost at the crack. "When I find you, I'm gonna make you watch while I skin this preacher alive! Then maybe you'll learn your place!"

Michelle's hand found mine in the darkness. "This way," she whispered. "The water sound — it gets louder where the tunnel opens out. Pa said it leads to a box canyon about a half-mile from here."

We moved as quickly as we dared in the absolute darkness, using the sound of flowing water as our guide. The tunnel floor was treacherous – slick with moisture and uneven.

Every few steps, Michelle would squeeze my hand in warning just before some obstacle: a sudden drop, a low-hanging formation, a sharp turn in the passage.

Behind us, we heard cursing as James discovered the crack. "Luke! Matthew! Get your worthless hides over here! There's another tunnel!"

"They won't fit," Michelle whispered with grim satisfaction. "The Carson brothers are too broad in the shoulder. Only James and maybe Cole can follow us through there."

She was right. We heard more cursing as the Carson brothers tried and failed to squeeze through the opening. But then came the sound we dreaded – James's voice, closer now, having made it through the crack.

"I can smell your fear, Michelle! Just like the night you found your daddy's letter.

Remember how that ended? Remember what happened to your mama's rose garden after I was done with you?"

I felt Michelle tense beside me, but her voice was steady when she spoke. "Keep moving. The tunnel starts to slope up soon – that means we're nearly there."

She was right again. The floor began to rise beneath our feet, and the air grew fresher. Somewhere ahead, I caught the faintest glimmer of pre-dawn light. We picked up our pace, hope lending us speed despite our exhaustion.

The sound of water grew louder, becoming a roar that echoed through the passage. The tunnel widened gradually, and the ceiling height increased until we could walk normally. The grey light ahead grew stronger, revealing the rough walls around us.

Then Michelle stopped abruptly, pulling me to a halt beside her. "Listen," she whispered.

For a moment, I heard nothing but the water. Then I caught it – the sound of horses above us, moving along the rim of what must be the box canyon she'd mentioned. "The Carson brothers," she said grimly. "They've ridden around to cut us off at the exit. They may not fit through the crack, but they're not stupid."

We stood in the semi-darkness, caught between James behind us and armed killers ahead. The situation seemed hopeless, but something in Michelle's stance told me she wasn't done fighting yet.

"Pa said there was another way," she said, feeling along the wall. "A chimney... a vertical shaft that the Comanche used to..." Her hand found something. "Here! Feel this air current?"

I placed my hand where she indicated and felt a steady stream of cool air flowing down from above.

Looking up, I could just make out a narrow shaft disappearing into darkness.

"It comes out in a thicket of scrub oak," Michelle explained quickly. "Above the canyon rim, but away from where the Carson brothers will be watching."

She pressed something into my hands – the packet containing her father's letter. "You go first. If anything happens to me, get these papers to Judge Richardson in Austin. Promise me." "We go together," I said firmly, echoing her words from earlier. "Or not at all."

The chimney was barely wide enough for a person, ascending at a steep angle into darkness. Years of water flow had worn handholds and footholds into the limestone – not comfortable, but manageable. The real challenge would be climbing in near-total darkness while injured and exhausted.

"I can hear them coming," Michelle whispered urgently. "Victor, please – you have to go first. The papers..." "Are staying right here with us," I interrupted, pressing them back into her hands. "Your father entrusted them to you, not me. Now, I'll give you a boost up, then follow. Together, remember?"

A shot rang out from the tunnel behind us, the bullet sparking off the rock wall. James's voice echoed through the passage, closer than ever. "Found their trail! They're cornered now!"

Without further argument, I laced my fingers together to make a stirrup for Michelle's foot. She stepped up, finding the first handholds in the shaft above. Despite the urgency of our situation, I couldn't help but admire her grace and strength as she began to climb.

"The holds are better than they look," she called down softly. "About ten feet up, there's a ledge where you can rest."

I started up after her, trying to ignore the burning pain in my grazed arm. The rock was slick with moisture, and more than once I nearly lost my grip. Above me, Michelle's quiet encouragement helped me find the next hold, the next step up.

We had reached the ledge she'd mentioned when lantern light flooded the tunnel below. James appeared, his face twisted with rage and drink. He raised his pistol, but the angle was awkward, and his shot went wide.

"You think this changes anything?" he shouted, his voice bouncing off the walls. "You think you can just disappear? I own half the lawmen in Texas! There's nowhere you can hide that I won't find you!"

"You don't own anyone anymore, James Morton!" Michelle's voice rang with conviction. "My father's letter will see to that!"

The effect of the name was immediate. James's face went pale, then purple with fury. "You stupid whore!" he screamed, firing wildly up the shaft. "I'll kill you like I killed your father!"

The confession echoed through the cave, clear as Sunday bells. Above us, we heard voices at the canyon rim – the Carson brothers, drawn by the shots and shouting.

"Keep climbing," Michelle urged. "There's another ledge just above us, then the shaft opens out near the surface." We climbed in desperate silence, feeling our way in the grey pre-dawn light that now filtered down from above. My arms trembled with exhaustion, and every movement sent fresh pain through my wounded arm. Below us, we could hear James struggling to climb the shaft, cursing with every step.

Michelle reached the upper ledge first. As she helped pull me up, loose rocks clattered down the shaft, followed by a cry of pain and rage from James. Looking down, I saw his lantern fall, shattering on the tunnel floor far below. Darkness swallowed the shaft again, broken only by the faint light from above.

"Almost there," Michelle whispered. "The opening's just ahead. But Victor..." She grabbed my arm, her grip urgent. "The Carson brothers will be watching. We'll only have seconds to reach the scrub oak before they see us."
I nodded, understanding the plan without words
. "Lead the way. I'll be right behind you." The final stretch of climbing was the hardest. The shaft narrowed even further, and the holds were less distinct. Every movement seemed to loosen more rocks, sending them clattering down toward our pursuer. James's curses grew more creative, but also more distant – he was falling behind. Finally, Michelle's head emerged into open air.

She pulled herself out quickly, then reached back to help me. As I crawled out of the shaft, the first rays of dawn were just touching the eastern sky.

We lay flat on the rocky ground, catching our breath. The scrub oak thicket was about thirty yards away, offering our only cover. Between us and safety was open ground, clearly visible from the canyon rim where the Carson brothers waited.

"Ready?" Michelle whispered, her hand finding mine.
"Together," I replied, squeezing her fingers.
We rose and ran, keeping low. Behind us, a shout went up from the canyon rim. Gunshots cracked across the morning air, bullets kicking up dust around our feet. But the Carson brothers had been watching the canyon exit, not the hidden shaft, and their angle was poor.

We reached the thicket just as James's head emerged from the shaft. His first shot caught the branch next to my head, sending bark flying. But by then we were through the scrub oak, running down the far side of the ridge where the morning shadows still held.

"The horses!" Michelle gasped as we ran. "Pa kept two emergency mounts in a box canyon near here. If they haven't found them..."

She led the way through the rough country, moving with the confidence of someone who'd grown up on this land. Behind us, the sounds of pursuit grew fainter – the horses our pursuers rode couldn't easily navigate this broken ground.

After what seemed like hours but was probably only minutes, we reached a narrow cleft in the rock. Hidden in the shadows were two horses, saddled and ready. Michelle's father had indeed thought of everything.

We mounted quickly, Michelle taking the lead as we picked our way through the rough country. By the time the sun cleared the horizon, we were miles away, heading east toward Arkansas and whatever future God had planned for us.

"They'll keep hunting us," Michelle said as we finally slowed our pace. "James – Morton – won't give up easily."

"Let them hunt," I replied, reaching over to take her hand. "We have truth on our side now, and your father's letter. And most importantly, we have each other."

She smiled then, a real smile that chased away the shadows of the night. "Together?"

"Together," I confirmed. "All the way to Arkansas and whatever comes after."

We rode on as the morning brightened around us, leaving the cave and its darkness behind. I didn't know then what trials still awaited us, what dangers we'd face before we reached safety. But I knew, with a certainty that went bone-deep, that God hadn't brought us this far to abandon us now.

Behind us, the sun rose over Texas, painting the sky in colors of hope and new beginnings. Somewhere back there, James Morton and his men were still searching, still cursing our escape. But they were searching for two people who no longer existed – the beaten-down wife and the naive preacher. In their place rode two survivors, stronger together than apart, ready to face whatever came next.

As we crossed a rise and saw the endless prairie stretching before us, Michelle began to sing softly – not a hymn this time, but a love song her father had taught her. The words floated back to me on the morning breeze, speaking of hope and courage and the kind of love that defies darkness.

I joined in as we rode, our voices blending like our lives had begun to do. The road ahead was long and uncertain, but we faced it together, carrying truth and justice like banners into the dawn of a new day.

CHAPTER 3:
ANOTHER DAY IN PARADISE

Spring mornings in Arkansas always reminded me of God's grace. Twenty years had passed since Michelle and I fled across Texas with nothing but faith and fear as companions. Now, watching the sun rise over our two hundred acres, I could hardly believe the life we'd built together.

The Lord had blessed us beyond measure, turning our desperate flight into a journey home.
The rooster's crow echoed across our land, followed by Michelle's familiar call: "Victor? Victor? Honey, it's time to get up and start the coffee."
"Yes, I know," I mumbled into my pillow, though we both knew I'd need another gentle reminder.

"You know I'm not even sure why we have these damned roosters! Cause you sure as hell don't wake up when they start squawking!"
I smiled into the darkness. "I know baby, but that's what I got you for, ain't it?"
Twenty years of marriage hadn't dimmed her spirit one bit. If anything, freedom had only made her stronger.

She'd grown into herself like a tree growing toward the sun, straight and true and beautiful. The scared woman I'd met at that revival was long gone, replaced by a matriarch who ran our household with grace and wisdom that amazed me daily.

As I stumbled to the kitchen to start the coffee, I couldn't help but thank God for everything He'd blessed us with. Even in the midst of the current depression gripping the country, we had everything we needed. The farm was thriving, our livestock healthy, and our gardens produced enough to help feed half the county's poor. But our greatest blessing was our children – seven daughters and three sons, each one a miracle in their own right.

Through the window above the sink, the sun painted the hills gold while the coffee brewed. The morning mist still clung to the valley, making our world look like something out of a dream. In the distance, I could see our oldest boy, John, already out checking the fence line. At seventeen, he was the spitting image of his grandfather – same strong jaw, same way of handling horses like they were dance partners. He had his mother's quiet strength too, though he showed it differently. The hands we hired called him the yard boss, always making sure everyone had their chores done proper.

The smell of biscuits drifting up from the summer kitchen told me Lilly was already at work. Our oldest at nineteen, she had her mama's grace and her daddy's calling to serve. Every morning, she was up before dawn, making sure her siblings would have a proper breakfast before their chores. She taught Sunday school, could quote scripture better than most of my deacons, and had half the eligible young men in the county walking into fence posts when she passed by. But Lilly had higher aspirations than marriage – she wanted to be a missionary, to carry the Word to places where it hadn't been heard.

The twins, Adrienne and Alley, would be up soon. At sixteen, they were as different as could be while still looking identical. Adrienne was our scholar, always with her nose in a book, dreaming of going to college back East. Alley was more practical, happiest when she was helping in the barn or working with the horses. But both had their mama's fire – Lord help anyone who tried to tell them what they couldn't do.

A melody drifted down from upstairs – Gabby practicing her hymns. Our fourteen-year-old had a voice like an angel and the patience to match. She was teaching her younger siblings to sing, turning our home into what Michelle called "a little piece of heaven's choir." Even now, I could hear little Grace's voice joining in, slightly off-key but full of joy.

Sarah, our twelve-year-old peacemaker, would be mediating between Rachel and James by now. Those two, at ten and thirteen, could fight over whether water was wet if you let them. But Sarah had a way about her that could calm any storm. "Just like her daddy," Michelle always said, though I knew that gift came from her mama's side. Thomas, fifteen and thoughtful, would be in his usual spot on the back porch, reading his Bible before breakfast.

He had my love for books and Michelle's gift with horses, a combination that made him particularly suited to help with both the farm and the ministry. People said he'd make a fine preacher someday, though he seemed more drawn to teaching than preaching.

"Are you going to stand there dreaming all morning, or is there coffee in my future?" Michelle's voice brought me back to the present. She stood in the doorway, fresh from gathering eggs, her silver-streaked hair catching the morning light. Twenty years had only made her more beautiful, adding wisdom to her grace and strength to her gentleness.

I poured her a cup of coffee, black and strong just like she liked it. "Just thinking about how blessed we are," I said, pulling her close. "Did you ever imagine, back in Texas, that we'd have all this?"

She smiled against my chest. "I didn't dare imagine anything past the next sunrise back then. But God had bigger plans than our fears, didn't He?"

Before I could answer, the house began to wake in earnest. Footsteps thundered down the stairs as our brood descended for breakfast. Lilly called from the summer kitchen that the biscuits were ready, and the peaceful morning erupted into our usual controlled chaos.

Grace, our youngest at eight, launched herself into my arms like she did every morning.

"Papa! Did you see the new calf? It's got a star on its head just like in my prayer!"

Rachel wasn't far behind, her words tumbling out in excitement. "Papa, can I ride into town with John today? Mrs. Henderson said she'd teach me to make lace if I helped in her shop, and I promised to be good, and…"

"After your chores," Michelle and I said in unison, a response worn smooth by years of practice.

The boys clattered in from their morning tasks, bringing the smell of horses and hay with them. John's quiet "Morning, Pa" was nearly lost under James's enthusiastic description of his latest invention – something to do with making the water pump work better, though I couldn't follow all the details.

Michelle moved through the chaos like a conductor leading an orchestra, making sure everyone had what they needed. She handed out chore assignments, settled disputes before they could start, and somehow managed to make each child feel specially noticed in the process.

"Adrienne, help your sister with the little ones' hair before breakfast. Alley, those boots are not coming to the table – back porch, now. Thomas, would you lead grace this morning? And Gabby, honey, save the high notes for church, please."

I watched her in amazement, as I did every morning. She caught my eye and winked, knowing exactly what I was thinking. Twenty years ago, she'd been a broken woman running for her life. Now she was the heart of our home, the strength that held us all together.

Breakfast was its usual organized riot – fifteen people around a table meant for twelve, passing plates and sharing stories about their dreams and plans.

Michelle had insisted from the start that we eat together as a family, no matter how cramped it got. "A family that prays together, stays together," she always said, "but a family that eats together, talks together."

Looking around that table, I saw God's grace made manifest. Each face reflected some combination of Michelle and me, but they were all uniquely themselves.

Lilly's quiet dignity, the twins' fierce independence, Gabby's joyful spirit, Sarah's gentle wisdom, Rachel's untamed energy, Grace's innocent faith. John's steady strength, Thomas's thoughtful nature, James's creative fire. Each one a gift, each one a miracle.

After breakfast, as the children scattered to their chores and studies, Michelle and I had our quiet moment on the front porch. It was our daily ritual – just a few minutes to share coffee and watch the sun climb over our little piece of paradise.

"The Henderson girl's getting married next month," Michelle said, settling into her rocking chair. "Sarah's already planning what she'll wear to the wedding."

"Twelve's a bit young to be thinking about weddings," I protested.

Michelle laughed. "Says the man who helped a strange woman run away after knowing her less than a week."

"That was different," I said, reaching for her hand. "That was God's plan."

She squeezed my fingers, her calloused palm warm against mine. "Yes, it was. And look what He did with it."

The morning light had barely touched the church steeple when I made my way down to my study. The white clapboard building stood proud against the Arkansas sky, twice the size it had been when we first arrived. Twenty years of ministry had grown our little congregation from thirty souls to over three hundred, and every expansion felt like a testament to God's faithfulness.

My study, a small room off the main sanctuary, was Michelle's gift to me on our tenth anniversary. She'd saved egg money for months to buy the oak desk that dominated the space, and the children had helped her line the walls

with bookshelves. Every morning, I spent an hour here in prayer and preparation before the day's work began.
"A minister needs his war room," Michelle always said, "a place to wrestle with God's Word before he delivers it to the people."

The morning sun streamed through the window, highlighting the worn leather of my Bible and the stack of letters requiring attention. Being the only minister for twenty miles meant more than just Sunday sermons. There were marriages to counsel, funerals to plan, disputes to mediate, and souls to tend. Each letter represented someone in need of guidance or comfort.

As I settled into my morning routine, I could hear Michelle in the main sanctuary, humming as she arranged flowers for Sunday's service. She'd turned the care of God's house into an art form, making sure every detail reflected the beauty of worship. The other women in town had started calling her the First Lady of the Church, though she'd laugh and say she was just the chief duster and flower arranger.

But she was so much more than that. Over the years, Michelle had built a network of care that reached every corner of our community. She organized the women's ministry, ran the Sunday School program, and somehow kept track of every birth, death, illness, and celebration in our congregation. People said she had a sixth sense about trouble – she'd show up with soup or bread just when a family needed it most.

"Remember what it was like to have nothing?" she'd say when I marveled at her energy. "God didn't bless us so we could keep it to ourselves."

A knock at the study door interrupted my thoughts. Deacon Thompson stood there, his weathered face serious. At seventy-two, he was one of our oldest church members and my closest advisor.

"Morning, Reverend Wright," he said, settling into the chair across from my desk. "Thought we might want to discuss the mission project before the committee meeting tonight."

The mission project was our most ambitious undertaking yet – a home for orphaned children, built on ten acres of church land. Michelle had been pushing for it for years, and finally, the congregation had caught her vision.

"Sarah brought in the latest figures," Thompson continued, pulling out a sheaf of papers.

"We've raised almost half the money we need. Your wife's idea about the quilting circle was inspired – those auction pieces brought in more than we expected."

I smiled, remembering how Michelle had organized the women into teams, each one creating a masterpiece to sell. She'd worked alongside them, her fingers flying over the fabric as she told stories about Jesus and his parables.

"Every stitch a prayer," she'd said, "every piece a blessing for a child in need."

"The boys from the logging camp want to donate labor," Thompson added. "Seems your ministry there has borne fruit."

That had been Michelle's idea too. Three years ago, she'd noticed how many young men came to town on weekends, looking for trouble to fill their loneliness. She'd suggested we start holding services at the camp itself, followed by Sunday dinner served by church ladies.

Now those same rough men were some of our most faithful supporters.

"God works in mysterious ways," I said, remembering how many of those loggers had found their way to Christ over plates of Michelle's fried chicken and biscuits.

Thompson nodded sagely. "That He does. Speaking of which, how many are you baptizing this Sunday?"

"Seven," I replied, joy filling my heart at the thought. "Including old Jack Wilson."

Thompson's eyebrows shot up. "The moonshiner? Well, if that ain't a miracle, I don't know what is."

Jack Wilson's conversion had been particularly sweet. He'd shown up at church one Sunday, still drunk from the night before, intending to cause trouble. But Michelle had spotted him before he could start anything, had him seated with a cup of coffee and a biscuit before he knew what hit him.

Now he was one of our most devoted members, using his old still site as a testimony to God's transforming power.

Our conversation was interrupted by the sound of children's voices – the Sunday school teachers arriving for their weekly preparation meeting. Michelle had started this tradition years ago, insisting that teaching children required as much preparation as preaching to adults.

"Better go see what my wife has planned for the young ones this week," I said, standing. "Last time she had them acting out David and Goliath, Mrs. Peterson's boy got a bit too enthusiastic with his sling."

Thompson chuckled as he gathered his papers. "That's what I love about this place, Reverend. It's alive with the Spirit. You and Sister Michelle have built something special here."

As we walked to the main sanctuary, I could see what he meant. The building was humming with activity – women arranging flowers, children practicing hymns, teachers preparing lessons. Michelle stood in the midst of it all, her silver-streaked hair caught in a neat bun, directing traffic like a general commanding troops.

She caught my eye and smiled, that same smile that had captured my heart two decades ago. In that moment, I saw her as others must see her – not just my wife and the mother of our children, but a force for good in our community, a vessel of God's grace.

"Victor," she called, "could you help Brother Marcus move these benches? We're setting up for the quilting circle this afternoon."

As I moved to help, I marveled at how naturally she balanced all her roles – wife, mother, minister's helper, community leader. She seemed to know instinctively what each person needed, whether it was a stern word or a gentle touch, a prayer or a practical solution.

The morning passed in a blur of activity. I counseled a young couple preparing for marriage, visited two sick members, and worked on Sunday's sermon. Michelle organized the women's prayer group, taught a cooking class for young brides, and somehow found time to help Widow Jenkins with her garden.

By afternoon, the church was filled with the rhythmic sound of needles and quiet conversation as the quilting circle worked on their latest project. Michelle moved among the women, offering encouragement and guidance, her own needle flashing in the sunlight that streamed through the windows.

"Remember, ladies," I heard her say, "every stitch is a prayer for the child who'll sleep under this quilt. We're not just making blankets – we're wrapping these little ones in God's love."

Watching her, I was struck again by how far we'd come from those desperate days in Texas. God had taken our fear and turned it into faith, our flight into foundation. We'd built more than just a church here – we'd built a community, a family of faith that extended far beyond our own children.

As the afternoon light began to fade, I retreated to my study to finish Sunday's sermon. Through the open door, I could hear Michelle leading the women in a hymn, their voices rising and falling like a gentle tide.

The words floated to me, familiar and comforting:
"Amazing grace, how sweet the sound
That saved a wretch like me…"

Twenty years ago, those words had been our comfort as we fled across Texas. Now they were our testimony, sung by a congregation that had become our extended family. God had indeed been good to us, turning our trials into triumph, our weakness into strength.

The afternoon sun was dipping toward the horizon when I headed home from the church. The sound of laughter drew me toward the barn, where I found a scene that perfectly captured our family life. John was teaching little Grace to ride, while the twins argued good-naturedly about the best way to break a horse. Thomas sat on a hay bale, reading aloud to Sarah and Rachel, while James tinkered with some mysterious contraption in the corner.

Gabby's voice floated down from the hayloft, where she was practicing hymns while doing her chores.
Lilly emerged from behind a stall, hay in her hair but dignity intact. "Papa! You're home early. Mama said to tell you supper will be ready soon, and she needs to discuss something about the orphanage project with you."
Looking at my oldest daughter, I saw so much of her mother in her bearing. Lilly had inherited Michelle's strength and grace, but tempered with a gentleness all her own.

At nineteen, she was already showing signs of the woman she would become – strong in faith, firm in conviction, and tender in spirit.

"John," I called out, "how's Grace doing with her riding?" My oldest son grinned, steadying the gentle mare his sister sat upon. "She's a natural, Pa. Just like Mama. Show him your posting trot, Gracie."

Grace beamed with pride as she demonstrated her newfound skill. At eight, she was our baby, but she had all the determination of her older siblings. Her golden curls bounced as she rode, reminding me of her mother's hair in the Texas sunlight so many years ago.

"Papa, watch this!" Rachel called from where she and Sarah were now attempting to teach their old dog new tricks. At ten, Rachel was our wild child, always pushing boundaries and asking questions that made the Sunday School teachers sweat. But she had a heart of gold, especially for animals and anyone she perceived as being treated unfairly.

Sarah, ever the peacemaker, was mediating between the twins again. At twelve, she had an old soul, always finding ways to smooth troubled waters. "Adrienne," she was saying, "Alley's right about the gentle approach working better, but your point about firm boundaries is good too. Why not try both?"

The twins, now sixteen, were a study in contrasts despite their identical appearance. Adrienne, with her books and dreams of college, was our scholar. She'd already started corresponding with schools back East, determined to be the first woman in our part of Arkansas to earn a university degree. Alley, on the other hand, was happiest in the barn or fields, working with her hands and helping run the farm. But they shared a fierce loyalty to each other and a determination that reminded me daily of their mother.

"Pa," James called from his corner, "come see what I've invented! It's a new kind of water pump that should make it easier for Mama to water her garden." At thirteen, our youngest son was constantly creating things, his mind working in ways that both amazed and bewildered me. Michelle said he had my look when deep in thought, but his innovative spirit was all his own.

Thomas closed his book – Shakespeare, I noticed, not his usual Bible study – and came to join me. At fifteen, he was growing into a thoughtful young man, equally at home discussing theology or breaking horses. "Pa," he said quietly, "I've been thinking about what you said about the revival circuit. I'd like to come with you this time, if you'll have me."

Before I could respond, Michelle's voice rang out from the house: "Supper time! Everyone wash up, and I mean properly this time, James Wright – I can see those grease stains from here!"

The organized chaos of ten children heading in for supper was a sight that never failed to warm my heart. They moved as a unit, the older ones naturally helping the younger, years of practice making the process smoother than you'd expect with such a large family.

Our dining room was a testament to family life – the massive table I'd built when the twins were born had been expanded three times as our family grew. The chairs were a mismatched collection, each with its own story. The one Lilly sat in had been a gift from the congregation when she was born.

The twins' chairs were made from wood salvaged from our first barn. Each child had helped sand and stain their own seat, making it truly theirs.

Michelle stood at the head of the table, ladling out soup into bowls that moved down the line with practiced efficiency. Her silver-streaked hair was coming loose from its bun, and a smudge of flour decorated her cheek, but she'd never looked more beautiful to me.

"Everyone settled?" she asked, though it was more command than question. "Thomas, would you return thanks?"

As Thomas prayed, I looked around at our children's bowed heads. Each one was so different, yet they formed a perfect whole. Lilly's quiet strength, the twins' fierce independence, Gabby's joyful spirit, Sarah's gentle wisdom, Rachel's untamed energy, Grace's innocent faith. John's steady leadership, Thomas's thoughtful nature, James's creative fire.

"Mama," Gabby said as we began eating, "I've been working on a new harmony for Sunday's special music. Would you listen after supper?"

"Of course, honey," Michelle replied. "And Adrienne, I saw that letter from Wellesley College came today. We'll talk about it after the dishes are done."

The conversation flowed naturally, each child sharing their day's achievements and concerns. James explained his new invention in detail that only Alley seemed to fully follow. Lilly spoke about her plans for the next Sunday School lesson. John reported on the state of the farm's north pasture.

"Remember," Michelle said during a brief lull, "tomorrow's Saturday, and you know what that means." A chorus of groans met her words. Our Saturday tradition of deep cleaning the house was not popular, but Michelle insisted that cleanliness was next to godliness, and a clean house was a testament to an ordered soul.
"Mama," Rachel ventured, "since I'm helping Mrs. Henderson in town…"

"Nice try, young lady," Michelle cut her off with a smile. "You'll do your share before you go. We all work together in this family."

That was our foundation – working together, supporting each other, each contributing to the whole. Michelle and I had decided early in our marriage that our home would be built on love, faith, and mutual responsibility. Each child had chores suited to their age and abilities, and all were expected to help with the younger ones.

After supper, the familiar rhythm of evening chores began. Dishes were washed and dried, animals were fed, younger children were bathed and readied for bed. Michelle moved through it all like a conductor leading an orchestra, each child knowing their part in the symphony of family life.

As the younger ones settled in for their bedtime stories –
Michelle never missed this ritual, no matter how busy the
day had been – I sat on the porch with our older children.
These evening conversations were precious times, when
guards came down and hearts opened.

"Pa," John said quietly, "I've been thinking about asking
Mary Henderson to court. Would you speak to her
father?"

Lilly looked up from her Bible study. "I want to talk to you
and Mama about the mission field. I've been praying, and I
feel called to serve."

These moments, these conversations, were the fruit of
twenty years of building a family on faith and love. Each
child was finding their path, guided by the values we'd
tried to instill, but making their own way in the world.
Later, after all the children were in bed, Michelle joined me
on the porch. The night was warm, filled with the sound of
crickets and the distant call of whippoorwills.

She settled into her rocking chair with a contented sigh.
"They're growing up so fast," she said softly. "Sometimes I
look at them and can hardly believe they're ours."
I reached for her hand in the darkness. "They're our
miracle, Michelle. Every one of them."

The nightmare came again that night, more vivid than
before. Four black wolves, larger than any natural beast,
circling our home under a blood-red moon. One wore a
suit and smoked a cigar, its yellow eyes gleaming with
malevolent intelligence.

The others dressed like ranch hands, but their movements were wrong – too fluid, too calculated. In the dream, I was away, always away, when they came.

I watched, helpless, as they destroyed everything we'd built. They trampled our crops, burned our barn, and then... then they entered our home. Michelle's screams echoed in my head as I jolted awake, sweat-soaked and shaking.

"Victor?" Michelle's hand was warm on my chest, anchoring me to reality. "The wolves again?"
I nodded, unable to speak for a moment. She knew about the dreams – we'd never kept secrets from each other – but I hadn't told her how much worse they'd gotten lately. How much more detailed. How much more real.

"Maybe it's stress about the revival circuit," she suggested, though I could hear the doubt in her voice. "You've been working too hard lately."

But we both knew it was more than that. The dreams had started a month ago, right after I'd received that strange letter from Texas. It had been unmarked, containing only a newspaper clipping about the death of Cole Matthews – James Morton's old friend and accomplice. The article mentioned that before dying, Matthews had spoken at length with a Texas Ranger about "old business in Arkansas."

I'd burned the clipping, not wanting to worry Michelle. We'd built a good life here, raised our children in peace. The past was the past, or so I'd thought. But now...

"I should stay home," I said, sitting up in bed. "The revival circuit can wait. Something doesn't feel right."

Michelle sat up too, lighting the bedside lamp. In its soft glow, I could see the concern in her eyes, but also that familiar determination. "Victor Wright, you listen to me. We've spent twenty years building a life on faith, not fear. I won't have you throwing away your ministry because of bad dreams."

"But if Morton…"

"If James Morton knows where we are, he's had twenty years to do something about it," she interrupted. "We're not those scared kids anymore. We have friends here, respect. The children are almost grown. He has no power over us anymore."

She was right, of course. She usually was. But something nagged at me, a feeling I couldn't shake. "At least let me send John with you and the younger children to your sister's while I'm gone. Just to be safe."

Michelle's sister lived in Little Rock, and we'd been planning to send the younger children there anyway while I was on the revival circuit. Michelle usually stayed home with the older ones, keeping the farm running in my absence.

"No," she said firmly. "I'm not running anymore, Victor. This is our home. The children have school, responsibilities. John needs to oversee the fall planting. The twins have their studies. Lilly's teaching Sunday

School. We can't just disappear because you had a bad dream."

As if summoned by our voices, there was a soft knock at the door. "Mama? Papa?" It was Grace, our youngest, probably awakened by another nightmare of her own. "Come in, sweet pea," Michelle called, her voice instantly shifting from steel to silk.

Grace padded in, clutching her worn rag doll. At eight, she was the image of Michelle when we'd first met, except for having my blue eyes. "I had a bad dream," she sniffled. "About wolves."

Michelle and I exchanged a sharp glance. "Wolves, honey?" Michelle asked carefully, making room for Grace between us.

"Big black ones," Grace nodded, climbing into bed. "They were trying to get into the house, but Mama wouldn't let them. She was brave, like David with Goliath."
My blood ran cold. Before I could respond, another figure appeared in the doorway – Thomas, looking troubled. "I heard voices," he said. "I… I had a dream too. About wolves."

One by one, our children appeared, drawn by some unseen force. Each one had experienced the same dream, with slight variations. John saw himself trying to fight off the wolves while his siblings ran. Lilly dreamed of trying to hide the younger ones in the church. The twins described the wolf in the suit, with its cigar and yellow eyes.

Michelle's face grew paler with each account, but her voice remained steady. "Well," she said finally, "looks like we're having a family sleepover. Everyone grab your blankets and pillows."

Soon our bedroom was full of children, pallets spread across the floor like we used to do during storms. Michelle moved among them, tucking blankets, offering comfort, singing softly until they fell asleep one by one.

When only we were awake, she turned to me. "Tomorrow," she whispered, "you'll go into town and send a telegram to the Texas Rangers. Ask about James Morton. Then we'll decide what to do."
I nodded, pulling her close. "I'm sorry, Michelle. I thought we were free of him."

"We are free," she said fiercely. "Whatever happens, he can't take that from us. We've built something here that's stronger than his hate."

Looking around at our sleeping children, I prayed she wasright. But the image of that wolf in the suit, with its burning yellow eyes and cruel smile, wouldn't leave my mind. And somewhere in the distance, too far to be sure, I thought I heard a wolf howl.

In the morning, I rode into town early, before most of the shops were open. The telegraph office would open at eight, operated by young Billy Henderson – Mary's brother and possibly our future son-in-law, if John had his way. As I waited for the office to open, I noticed something odd. Three strangers were sitting outside the saloon, despite the early hour. They were dressed like cowboys, but something about them seemed wrong. One was smoking a cigar, the smoke curling up like a snake in the morning air.

When Billy finally arrived to open the office, I sent two telegrams. One to the Texas Rangers, asking about James Morton. The other to my contact in Little Rock, asking him to prepare a safe house. Just in case.

But as I mounted my horse to head home, I caught a glimpse of movement in the alley beside the telegraph office. One of the strangers was there, watching me. And in his hand, barely visible, was a crisp new telegram form. The week before my departure for the revival circuit passed with an eerie mix of normalcy and tension. On the surface, our daily routines continued – children doing their chores, Michelle running the household, me tending to church matters. But underneath, something had shifted. Like the heavy air before a storm, we could all feel it coming.

I'd received no response from the Texas Rangers, but the strangers in town had disappeared as mysteriously as they'd appeared. Billy Henderson claimed no knowledge of their telegram, though his nervous manner suggested otherwise. Michelle insisted we carry on as usual, not wanting to frighten the children more than they already were.

"We can't live in fear," she said one evening, as we sat on the porch watching the sunset. "If we do that, he's already won."

But I noticed she'd started keeping the younger children closer to home. Grace was no longer allowed to play in the far pasture. Rachel's trips to town were always accompanied now. Even the older ones had their movements restricted, though Michelle framed it carefully as extra chores needing attention.

John had taken to carrying his rifle when he checked the fence lines, and the twins kept their horses saddled day and night "just in case." Thomas spent hours in the barn with James, helping him design elaborate locks for the doors and windows. Only Lilly seemed unchanged, her faith providing a steady calm that helped anchor the younger ones.

Three days before I was set to leave, Michelle pulled me aside after supper. The children were in the barn for evening chores, and her face was grave in the fading light. "I found this in Grace's room," she said, holding out a piece of paper. It was a child's drawing, done in bold strokes of charcoal. Four wolves surrounded our house, one wearing what looked like a suit. In the background, a figure on horseback rode away – me, presumably.

"She says she sees them when she's awake now," Michelle continued, her voice steady but her hands trembling. "Not just in dreams. She says they're watching us from the woods."

I started to speak, but she pressed on. "Victor, I know what you're going to say. But we can't run. This is our home. These children have never known any other life. If we run now, we'll be running forever."

"Then let me stay," I pleaded. "The revival can wait."
"No," she said firmly. "We can't let fear rule us. You have a calling, a ministry. People are counting on you. Besides," she managed a small smile, "I'm not that scared little girl from Texas anymore. I can handle James Morton."
"Michelle…"

"I've already taken precautions," she continued. "John knows where all the papers are – property deeds, bank documents, your life insurance. Lilly knows how to contact my sister if… if anything happens. The twins have a plan to get the younger ones to safety if needed. And this…" she pressed a sealed envelope into my hands. "This is for Judge Richardson in Little Rock. If anything happens while you're gone, John knows to get it to him."

I looked at my wife in the gathering darkness, seeing both the scared young woman I'd rescued and the strong matriarch she'd become. "I love you," I said, pulling her close. "More than I did twenty years ago, if that's possible."

"Then trust me," she whispered against my chest. "Trust that God didn't bring us this far to abandon us now."
The next two days passed in a blur of preparation. I packed my saddlebags with sermons and my traveling Bible, while Michelle prepared food for my journey. The children were subdued, helping with preparations but unusually quiet. Even Rachel's normal exuberance was dampened.

The night before I was to leave, Michelle insisted on having a family dinner that was more feast than meal.

She'd prepared all our favorites – fried chicken, fresh bread, apple pies. The dining room was full of laughter and talk, everyone deliberately avoiding mention of tomorrow's departure or the shadows that seemed to lurk at the edges of our happiness.

After supper, we gathered in the parlor for family worship, another of Michelle's unbreakable traditions. Each child chose a favorite hymn, and Gabby played the piano while we sang. Grace wanted "Amazing Grace," the first hymn she'd learned to sing.

Rachel chose "Standing on the Promises," while Sarah requested "It Is Well with My Soul."
When it was Michelle's turn, she chose the hymn we'd sung at our wedding:
"Be not dismayed whate'er betide,
God will take care of you;
Beneath His wings of love abide,
God will take care of you."

Her voice was strong and clear, carrying the promise of those words into the gathering darkness outside our windows. The children's voices joined in, creating a harmony that seemed to push back against the shadows. Later, after the younger ones were in bed, I found Michelle in our room, packing some last-minute items in my bags.

She'd included small gifts from each child – a drawing from Grace, a whittled cross from James, a handwritten psalm from Thomas, pressed flowers from Rachel and Sarah, a handkerchief embroidered by the twins, a small book of prayers from Lilly, and a carved horse from John.

"So you'll have a piece of each of them with you," she explained, her voice catching slightly.

I held her then, memorizing everything about the moment – the scent of her hair, the strength of her embrace, the sound of our children's quiet movements in the house around us.

Something told me to stay, to forget the revival circuit and keep my family close. But Michelle was right – we couldn't let fear rule us.

That night, I dreamed again of the wolves. But this time, Michelle faced them with a fiery sword, like the angel guarding Eden. "You have no power here," she declared, her voice ringing with authority. "This is God's ground."

I woke before dawn to find Michelle already up, making coffee and biscuits for my journey.

The children appeared one by one, helping with morning chores in unusual silence. Even Grace seemed to understand the gravity of the moment.

As I mounted my horse, Michelle handed me a final package. "Your favorite cornbread," she said with a smile that didn't quite reach her eyes. "And Victor? Remember – whatever happens, you did the right thing twenty years ago. Never doubt that."

I looked at my family gathered in the early morning light – my beautiful, strong wife; our ten amazing children; the home we'd built together. "I'll be back in three weeks," I promised. "Take care of each other."

"God will take care of us," Michelle replied firmly. "He always has."

As I rode away, they started singing – Michelle's clear voice leading them in "God Be with You Till We Meet Again." I kept my eyes forward, not daring to look back, not knowing it would be the last time I'd see them alive.

The night James Morton came for my family, the moon hung blood-red in the sky. Later, witnesses would say it was just an ordinary harvest moon, but those who survived that night knew different. Evil had come to our quiet corner of Arkansas, wearing a suit and smoking a cigar, just as Grace had drawn it.

Michelle was in the kitchen when they first arrived, teaching Gabby and Sarah how to make their grandmother's bread recipe. The twins were studying in the parlor, while Lilly helped the younger ones with their lessons. John and Thomas were in the barn, and James was tinkering with his latest invention on the back porch.

The first warning came from the dogs – their usual barking suddenly silenced in a way that made Michelle's blood run cold. She would later be described as perfectly calm as she set the bread aside and gathered her children.

"Lilly," she said quietly, "get the little ones into the cellar. You remember what we discussed."

Lilly nodded, her face pale but determined. "Come on, Grace, Rachel. We're going to play that hiding game Mama taught us."

The sound of hooves in the yard – too many for casual visitors, especially this late. Michelle moved to the window, careful to stay hidden behind the curtain. Four riders approached the house, their shapes dark against the red moon. The leader sat his horse like a king, a cigar glowing in the darkness.

"My God," Michelle whispered, then immediately straightened her spine. "Adrienne, Alley – get your father's rifle and the shotgun. Gabby, Sarah – help Lilly with the little ones."

"Mama?" Thomas's voice came from the back door. "There are men in the barn. They've got John."
Michelle's face hardened. "James," she called softly to her youngest son, still on the back porch, "run to the Henderson place. Fast as you can, straight through the woods.

Tell them to get the sheriff."

But before James could move, a shot rang out. The boy fell forward, blood blooming on his shirt like a crimson flower.

"Now, now, Michelle," a familiar voice called from the darkness. "That's no way to treat a reunion. Send the rest of them out, nice and peaceful, and maybe we can discuss old times."

Twenty years had roughened James Morton's voice, but hadn't changed its cruel essence. Michelle pushed Thomas toward the cellar entrance. "Go," she whispered. "Protect your sisters."

"Mama, no —"

"Do as I say." Her voice held no argument. "The Lord is our shepherd," she began.

"I shall not want," Thomas finished, tears streaming down his face as he descended the cellar steps.

Michelle moved to the front door, opening it with steady hands. James Morton stood on her porch, looking older but no less dangerous. His suit was expensive, his smile cold as winter.

"Hello, darling," he said, blowing cigar smoke in her face. "Miss me?"

"Like I miss the slavery of Egypt," Michelle replied, her voice steady. "What do you want, James?"

"Now is that any way to greet your lawful husband?" His smile widened. "I want what's mine — you, this property, and twenty years of interest."

Behind him, the Carson brothers emerged from the barn, dragging John between them.

Her oldest son was bloody but conscious, his eyes meeting hers with silent apology. "You have no claim here," Michelle said.

"This is our home, bought with honest work and God's blessing."

Morton laughed, the sound like breaking glass. "Honest work? Is that what you call stealing another man's wife? Running with a preacher who turned out to be quite the wealthy land baron?"

His face hardened. "Where is the good Reverend Wright, by the way? I so looked forward to discussing scripture with him."

"Gone," Michelle said simply. "And you'll be gone too, James Morton. The sheriff –"

"Is currently occupied with a series of mysterious fires in town," Morton interrupted. "Seems several buildings caught fire all at once. Tragic, really. Now, about those other children…"

Michelle's hand moved slightly, and Morton's gun appeared as if by magic. "Careful, darling. I'd hate to make young John here an only child. Although," he glanced at James's still form on the porch, "I suppose he already is." What happened next would be pieced together later from various accounts. Michelle, it seemed, had been slowly moving her hand toward the shotgun hidden by the door.

Morton saw her intention and fired, but she was faster than he remembered. Her shot caught him in the shoulder, spinning him backward.

The Carson brothers opened fire, forcing Michelle back into the house. John used the distraction to break free, running toward the cellar entrance. He almost made it. The next few minutes were chaos. Shots rang out from multiple directions. The twins, it seemed, had been better shots than anyone knew, taking down one of the Carson brothers before being overwhelmed.

Gabby died trying to protect Sarah. Lilly was found later in the cellar, having used her body to shield Grace and Rachel.

Michelle's last stand was in the kitchen, where she'd made bread with her daughters just hours before. She'd barricaded the cellar door, giving Thomas time to lead the surviving younger children through the tunnel that James had helped dig "just in case." Her final shots emptied her husband's rifle, each one finding its mark.

But in the end, James Morton's evil prevailed. When he finally broke through the barricade, he found Michelle waiting, her father's Bible in her hands.

"The Lord is my shepherd," she began.

The shot cut off her prayer, but witnesses say she died with a smile on her face, knowing her youngest children had escaped.

Morton's rage at finding the cellar tunnel was terrible to behold. He ordered the house searched, then burned. Eight bodies were found – Michelle, John, the twins, Gabby, Sarah, Lilly, and James. Grace and Rachel were missing, along with Thomas.

But Morton's victory would be short-lived. For in his rage and drunken celebration, he made a crucial mistake. He left evidence. Evidence that would eventually point not to Victor Wright, but to himself.

I was three days into the revival circuit when God's voice woke me from a dead sleep. It wasn't a thunderous declaration or a burning bush – just a simple, undeniable command: "Go home." The moon outside my window was blood-red, and somewhere in the distance, wolves howled.

I rode through the night, pushing my horse harder than I should have. Dawn was breaking when I crested the hill overlooking our valley. The sight stopped my heart mid-beat. Where our home should have been, smoke rose in lazy curls against the morning sky. The barn was a blackened skeleton, and the house… The house was gone.

Emergency wagons were scattered across our yard, and a crowd had gathered – neighbors, church members, the sheriff's men. As I rode closer, their voices fell silent. Men removed their hats. Women turned away, wiping tears. No one would meet my eyes.

Deacon Thompson was the one who stepped forward. His weathered face was wet with tears, his voice rough with smoke and grief. "Reverend Wright… Victor… I'm so sorry. We tried to get here in time, but…"

"Michelle?" My voice sounded strange to my own ears. "The children?"

He shook his head slowly. "Eight bodies found so far. Michelle… the older ones… They fought like lions, son. Like lions."

The world tilted sideways. I would have fallen if John Henderson hadn't caught me. "Thomas?" I managed. "Grace? Rachel?"

"Missing," the sheriff said, stepping forward. "Along with the men who did this. We've got posses out searching, but…"

I barely heard him. I was moving toward the ruins of my home, drawn by some terrible need to see. The kitchen walls still stood partially, and I could smell fresh bread – Michelle's last act of normalcy before hell arrived. A charred quilt lay in the yard, one the twins had helped make for the orphanage. John's rifle, bent and blackened, lay near the barn where he'd made his last stand.

"Victor." Deacon Thompson's hand was on my shoulder. "There's something else. The men who did this… they left something. In the church."

The church stood untouched, pristine white against the smoke-darkened sky. Inside, the morning light filtered through stained glass windows Michelle had helped design. Everything was exactly as we'd left it – except for the altar. On the communion table lay my wife's Bible, open to Psalm 23. Beside it was a cigar, still smoldering, and a note written in a hand I hadn't seen in twenty years:

"Property always returns to its rightful owner. – J.M."

The rage that filled me then was like nothing I'd ever known. It burned away the gentle preacher, the loving father, leaving something else in its place. Something that understood, finally, what my nightmares had been trying to tell me.

"Victor," the sheriff said from behind me, "I have to ask… these men who did this… there's talk of an old connection to you and Michelle. Something from Texas?"

I turned slowly. The morning light caught the badge on his chest, making it gleam like judgment. "Are you asking me something specific, Sheriff?"

He shifted uncomfortably. "There's been a telegram from Texas. About a man named Morton. They say… they say he's claiming you killed his wife and children. That this was revenge for his family."

The laugh that came from my throat didn't sound human. "His wife? Is that what he's claiming? Let me tell you about James Morton…"

But before I could continue, young Billy Henderson burst into the church. "Reverend! They found something – in the cellar tunnel. Tracks leading out. Three sets."

Hope flared like lightning. Thomas, Grace, Rachel – they might have escaped. Might even now be making their way to Michelle's sister in Little Rock, just as we'd planned. But Morton would be hunting them too.

"Sheriff," I said, my voice steady now, "My surviving children are out there somewhere, running for their lives. The man who murdered their mother and siblings is hunting them. Now, you can either help me find them, or you can try to arrest me. But if you choose the second option, I should warn you – I'm not the same man who came to Arkansas twenty years ago."

The sheriff studied my face for a long moment. Then he sighed and pulled out a wanted poster. It showed James Morton's face, twenty years younger but unmistakable. "This came with the telegram from Texas. Seems Mr. Morton has quite a history of marrying women, killing their families, and taking their property. Texas Rangers have been building a case for years." "And now?" I asked. "Now we have fresh bodies, witnesses who saw him here, and evidence he can't explain away."

The sheriff's face hardened. "I've got three daughters myself, Reverend. You do what you need to do. Just… leave enough of him for the law to hang."
I nodded once, then walked out of the church and toward my horse. Behind me, I heard Deacon Thompson ask,

"Where are you going, Reverend?"

"To find my children," I replied without turning. "And then I'm going to kill James Morton.
"

"Victor," he called after me, "what about turning the other cheek? What about vengeance belonging to the Lord?"
I stopped, looking back at the smoke rising from my destroyed home.

At the sheet-covered forms being loaded into wagons. At the place where James had fallen, where Gabby had died protecting Sarah, where Lilly had given her life for her younger sisters.

"Sometimes," I said quietly, "God needs a willing vessel for His vengeance. And I aim to be that vessel.I mounted my horse and rode toward Little Rock, toward my surviving children, toward a reckoning twenty years in the making. Behind me, the sun rose fully, painting the sky the color of blood and judgment
Paradise was lost.
But I would make sure James Morton never found his.

CHAPTER 4:
THE SHEPHERD'S WRATH

The morning after I found my family murdered, I stood in what remained of our kitchen, watching the sun rise through the charred beams of our home.

Michelle had taught all our girls to bake in this kitchen. The twins had learned their mother's biscuit recipe right where I stood. Now the floor was stained with blood that no amount of rain would ever wash away.

"Reverend Wright?" Deacon Thompson's voice came from behind me. "The search parties are ready."

I nodded without turning. In my hand, I held the remains of Grace's rag doll, found near the cellar entrance. The fabric was scorched but still recognizable – Michelle had made it from scraps of the dress she'd worn when we fled Texas.

"We found tracks," Thompson continued. "Three sets, heading east. Thomas must have remembered the escape route you and Michelle planned."

Of course Thomas remembered. He was our thoughtful one, always planning, always preparing. Just like his mother.

"The trail's clear enough," Thompson added. "If we leave now—"

"No." My voice sounded strange even to me. "You organize the search parties. I hunt alone."

"Victor," Thompson's voice took on the counseling tone he'd used so often during church meetings. "You're not thinking clearly

. You're a minister, not a—"

"Not anymore." I turned to face him, and something in my expression made him step back. "The minister died with his family. What's left is just a father looking for his children. And a husband with a debt to pay."

I walked past him, out into the morning light. The yard was still full of neighbors and lawmen, all watching me with a mixture of pity and uncertainty. They'd known me for twenty years as their gentle preacher, the man who quoted scripture and counseled turning the other cheek. That man was gone.

John Henderson approached, leading my horse. The animal was still tired from our desperate ride home, but it would have to serve.

"Billy's been monitoring the telegraph office," John said quietly. "No word about the children, but..." he hesitated.
"Speak plain, John. I buried most of my family yesterday. There's nothing you can say that can hurt me now."
"Morton's been seen near Little Rock. He's got men watching the roads, and..." John swallowed hard. "He's offering rewards for information about Thomas and the girls. Living or dead."

My hand tightened on Grace's doll. "How many men ride with him?"
"Reports vary. Six, maybe eight. The Carson brother who survived the fight here is with them."
I mounted my horse, checking my weapons.

Michelle had never liked guns in our home, but she'd insisted we keep them clean and ready. "A shepherd needs teeth to fight wolves," she'd said. Now her wisdom would serve a different purpose.

"Victor," Thompson called from the porch. "Remember Psalms: 'Vengeance is mine, sayeth the Lord.'"
I turned in my saddle to face him. "Read your Bible closer, Deacon. Sometimes the Lord works through willing vessels."

The sun was fully up now, painting the sky the color of fresh blood. I rode east, following tracks only a father's eyes could see. Thomas had led his sisters into the woods, avoiding the main roads just as Michelle and I had taught them. Smart boy. He would have kept Grace quiet, let Rachel scout ahead. They would be making for their aunt's house in Little Rock, but taking the long way to avoid pursuit.

Unless Morton found them first.
The thought spurred me faster. The countryside passed in a blur as I pushed my horse harder than was wise. Memories ambushed me at every turn – this was where John had learned to ride, there was where the twins had their secret meeting place, up ahead was the creek where I'd baptized Lilly.

Now John lay dead in the fresh-turned earth behind our burned-out home. The twins would never again finish each other's sentences or argue about horses. Lilly would never realize her dream of being a missionary.

But three might still live. Three might yet be saved. Around noon, I found their first real sign – a torn piece of Rachel's dress caught on a bramble. The fabric was dirty but free of blood. Nearby, partially hidden under leaves, I found evidence they'd stopped to rest – a heel print in soft earth, a broken cracker, three distinct sets of tracks leading onward.

They were alive. Moving tired but purposeful. Thomas was leading them well.

A shot rang out, the bullet kicking up dirt near my horse's hooves. I dismounted smoothly, drawing my gun as I moved behind a tree.

"That was a warning," a rough voice called. "Next one goes through your head, preacher man."
I recognized the voice – Luke Carson, the surviving brother. The one who'd helped murder my family.
"Funny," I called back, "I was about to say the same to you."

A harsh laugh. "You? The peaceful preacher? Way I hear it, you ain't shot anything bigger than a rabbit in twenty years."

I listened carefully, tracking his voice. He was moving, trying to circle around. Amateur's mistake.
"Think what you like," I replied. "But ask yourself this – what's a man got to lose when you've already killed his family?"

Another shot, closer now. Luke was getting cocky. "You gonna quote scripture at me, Reverend? Pray for my soul?" I smiled, but there was no joy in it. "No, Mr. Carson. I'm going to send you to meet your brother."

He fired again, and I had him. Moving fast, I came around the tree. Two shots rang out almost as one. Luke's went wild. Mine didn't.

He lay in the leaves, blood spreading across his chest, eyes wide with surprise. "You... you ain't no preacher," he gasped.

"Not anymore." I knelt beside him. "Now, you're going to tell me where Morton's headed. Where he plans to intercept my children."
"Go to hell."

I pressed my thumb into his wound. "After you. And I've got some time before you bleed out. Your choice how you spend it."

His eyes widened further, seeing something in my face that scared him more than dying. "Little Rock," he gasped. "Morton's got... got men watching every road. But... but that ain't all..."

"Speak plain," I commanded, pressing harder.
"Morton ain't working alone," Luke coughed. "Got friends here... important friends... been planning this for..."
His eyes glazed over before he could finish. I searched his body, finding a sealed letter addressed to James Morton.

The contents confirmed my worst fears – Morton had friends in Little Rock, people of influence. The conspiracy ran deeper than I'd imagined.

I buried Luke Carson shallow, not from any Christian charity but because I didn't want wild animals dragging pieces of him where my children might see. As I worked, I thought about his last words. Important friends. A long-planned conspiracy.

Someone had told Morton exactly when I'd be away. Someone had made sure Billy Henderson wouldn't warn me about the telegram. Someone had been watching my family, learning their routines, finding the perfect time to strike.

But who? And more importantly, why wait twenty years? The sun was westering when I mounted up again. I'd lost time with Carson, but gained valuable information. Morton wasn't just hunting my children – he was herding them toward Little Rock. Toward a trap.
Unless I got there first.

I rode hard through the afternoon, following my children's trail. They were moving smart but slow – Thomas couldn't push the girls too hard. Grace was only eight, and Rachel, for all her spirit, was still just ten. They would need rest, food, shelter.

Just before sunset, I found their campsite from the night before – carefully hidden, all traces of fire buried, just as Michelle and I had taught them. Thomas had used every lesson we'd ever given about survival. My heart swelled with pride even as it ached with worry.

As I prepared to make my own camp, movement caught my eye. A rider on the ridge above, silhouetted against the dying sun. Even at this distance, I recognized the shape – Deacon Thompson, who was supposed to be coordinating search parties in the opposite direction.

What was he doing out here, alone?

The question nagged at me as darkness fell. Something wasn't right. Too many coincidences, too many convenient explanations.

As I sat in the gathering dark, I took out Michelle's Bible – the one Morton had left on the church altar. A paper fell from between its pages, covered in my wife's neat handwriting. A list of names, dates, and… my blood ran cold. At the top of the page, in Michelle's hand: "People we can't trust." The first name on the list: Deacon Samuel Thompson.

Michelle's list burned in my pocket as I rode through the night. The moon was full now, no longer blood-red but sharp as judgment against the black sky. My wife had known – had suspected something was wrong long before that final night. Why hadn't she told me?

But I knew why. Michelle had always protected me, especially from things that might shake my faith in people. "You need to trust to be a good minister," she'd say. "Let me worry about the wolves."

The list had five names. Thompson's was first, followed by four others I recognized from our community. All men of standing, all people I'd trusted. All people who had helped us build our life here.

Or helped us build the illusion of a life.
Dawn found me at the edge of Miller's Creek, where another set of tracks joined my children's trail. Horses – at least three riders, moving parallel to Thomas's path. They weren't trying to catch up, just… following. Herding.
"Thought I might find you here."

I turned to find John Henderson riding up, his rifle across his saddle. The morning light showed his face gray with exhaustion.

"You shouldn't have followed me," I said.
"Maybe not." He dismounted, checking the tracks himself. "But Mary made me promise. Said she owes it to Miss Michelle."

I studied him carefully. John had grown up with my children, been sweet on Mary Henderson since they were twelve. His father had been our first friend in Arkansas.
"What aren't you telling me, John?"
He wouldn't meet my eyes. "Billy… he didn't just hide that telegram. There were others. Been coming for months. Thompson made him…"
"Made him how?"
"The bank." John's voice was bitter.

"Thompson's been buying up loans all over the county. Owns half the town's debts now. Including the Henderson's store."

Another piece clicked into place. Thompson hadn't just been our deacon – he'd been quietly building power, gathering leverage over the whole community.
"There's more," John added. "That night... the fires in town that kept the sheriff away? They weren't random. I saw Thompson talking to the men who started them. Gave them money right there in the street."

Rage rose in my throat, hot as bile. While my family was being slaughtered, Thompson had made sure no help would come.

A shot cracked across the creek. John's horse went down, screaming. We dove for cover as more bullets kicked up dirt around us.

"Four of them," John whispered, chambering a round. "Up on the ridge."

I'd already counted them. Morton's men, by their shooting style – spraying bullets, hoping to get lucky. Luke Carson had been a better shot than these ones.
"Give it up, Reverend!" One called. "Morton just wants to talk!"

"Like he talked to my wife?" I called back. "My children?"
"That was business. This is different."

"You're right about that." I picked up a stone, tossed it to the left. As they fired at the movement, I rolled right and came up shooting.

The first man died before he knew I'd moved. The second had time for one wild shot before my bullet took him in the throat. The third tried to run and died for it.

The fourth threw down his gun. "Don't shoot! Please! I can tell you things!"

I approached him carefully, John covering me. The man was young, barely more than a boy. His hands shook as he raised them.

"Start talking," I said.

"Morton's got a place outside Little Rock," he babbled. "Old plantation house. That's where they're taking your kids when they catch them. Thompson's been helping set it up for months. They got papers… papers saying you killed Morton's family back in

Texas. Gonna use them to take everything you own."

"What papers?"

"I don't know! Thompson handles all that. Him and some judge in Little Rock. They're gonna make it look like you went crazy, killed your family 'cause they found out about your past crimes."

I thought of Michelle's list. Was the judge's name on it?

"Please," the boy begged. "That's all I know. I just needed the money. My sister's sick and—"

The shot took him in the back of the head. He fell forward, revealing Deacon Thompson on the ridge behind him, rifle still smoking.

"Loose ends," Thompson called down. "Bad for business."

I fired, but he was already gone, disappearing into the trees like the snake he was. John cursed beside me.

"My horse is done for," he said. "And they'll have others waiting ahead."

I handed him my reins. "Take my horse. Ride back, warn the sheriff what's really happening. And John?" I caught his arm. "Check on your family. Get them somewhere safe."

"What about you?"

"I'm going hunting."

He nodded once, understanding. As he mounted up, he turned back. "Victor? Miss Michelle… she knew something was wrong. Last month, she came to the store, asked my mother to keep some papers safe. Said if anything happened…"

"Where are they?"

"Hidden in the store's cellar. Behind the north wall."

Another piece of Michelle's planning. Even in death, she was protecting us.

After John rode out, I searched the bodies. More letters, more proof of Thompson's involvement. One carried a detailed map of the area, showing multiple routes to Little

Rock. They'd planned to trap my children no matter which way they ran.

But Thomas was smarter than they'd expected. The tracks showed he'd crossed the creek upstream, then doubled back. He was using every trick Michelle and I had taught him about avoiding pursuit.

Still, he was just fifteen, trying to protect two young sisters. He'd need rest eventually. Need help.

I studied the map, seeing what they'd planned. The old plantation house had to be Willow Grove – abandoned since the war, remote enough for their purposes. If I moved fast, cut across country…

Movement in the trees caught my eye. A flash of blue – Rachel's dress? No, too high up. A signal flag, barely visible through the branches. Someone was watching, coordinating the pursuit.

I moved through the woods like a shadow, all those hunting trips with John finally serving their purpose. As I got closer, I could make out a figure in the trees – another of Morton's men, using flags to signal someone further ahead.

He never heard me coming. As he fell, I caught his signal book. The codes were simple enough to break – directions, numbers of pursuers, locations of checkpoints.

And there, on the last page, tomorrow's instructions in Thompson's handwriting: "Drive them toward the river. M. will be waiting at Carter's Ford."

My children were being herded into a trap, and I was a day behind. But now I knew where they were headed. Knew who was really behind it all.

I stopped only long enough to bury Michelle's list in a hollow tree, marking it so I could find it again. If anything happened to me, someone would need to know the truth. As I moved through the woods, I thought about Thompson sitting in our church, praying with us, breaking bread at our table. Twenty years of lies. Twenty years of plotting our destruction.

And somewhere ahead, James Morton waited to destroy what was left of my family.
The shepherd's crook, they say, was first made to guide sheep. But it was also made to break wolves' necks.
It was time to show Thompson and Morton what happened when shepherds went to war.
The abandoned church rose from the morning mist like a ghost of better days.

Its white paint had long since weathered to gray, and vines climbed the empty bell tower where I'd once preached during a revival circuit. Standing in the pre-dawn light, watching fog curl around its weathered foundations, I remembered Michelle's words the first time we'd used this place as a waypoint: "God's houses are never truly abandoned, Victor. They just wait for those who need sanctuary."

My boots made no sound on the overgrown path leading to the front steps. Twenty years of Arkansas weather had taken its toll on the building, but it still stood proud against the wilderness trying to reclaim it. Michelle's network of faithful women had maintained it as best they could, using it as one of many safe houses in a chain stretching toward Little Rock.

The door hung slightly ajar – the first sign something was wrong. Thomas knew better than to leave such an obvious trail. I drew my gun before mounting the steps, each weathered board a potential betrayer ready to creak under my weight. But Michelle's friends had kept the stairs solid, and I reached the entrance in silence.

Inside, the church still smelled of old hymnals and forgotten prayers. Dust motes danced in the weak light filtering through broken stained glass, and the remains of the old altar stood like a faithful sentinel at the far end. But it was the floor that told the story I needed to read. Three sets of footprints in the dust. Small ones – Grace's – staying close to larger ones that could only be Thomas's. Rachel's wandered more, showing her restless spirit even in flight. They'd come here following the escape route Michelle and I had planned years ago, seeking supplies and shelter on their way to Little Rock

.

But something had gone wrong. The footprints showed panic, sudden movement. By the altar, signs of a struggle scarred the ancient floorboards. And there, sprawled before God's table, lay one of Morton's men – dead by the knife I'd given Thomas for his thirteenth birthday. My gentle, thoughtful son had killed a man in God's house. The knowledge sat like lead in my stomach as I knelt to examine the scene. The fight had been desperate, uneven.

Thomas had been protecting his sisters, fighting like a cornered wolf despite his youth. Like father, like son – though this was a legacy I'd never wanted to pass on. Moving deeper into the church, I found signs of their hasty departure. They'd abandoned supplies they desperately needed – food, water, the warm blankets Michelle's friends had stored here. Something had spooked them badly enough to flee without vital provisions.

Behind the altar, the hidden compartment where supplies were kept stood open. Inside, I found fresh ammunition and – my heart jumped – a letter addressed to me in Michelle's handwriting.

But before I could read it, a sound from outside froze me in place.

Horses approaching. Multiple riders, trying to be quiet and almost succeeding. They'd followed the same trail I had, but with less care for silence. I moved to the broken window, staying in shadow.

James Morton sat his horse at the edge of the trees, looking exactly as Grace had drawn him – the wolf in a suit, cigar smoke curling around him like a demon's breath. Eight riders spread out at his gesture, moving to surround the church.

But it was the tenth figure that made my blood run cold. Billy Henderson stood beside Morton's horse, rifle in hand, face pale with fear or shame. The boy who'd grown up with my children, who'd mooned after Mary at Sunday socials, who'd helped teach Grace to read – now stood with the men who'd murdered my family.

The betrayals, it seemed, would never end.

I touched Michelle's unread letter in my pocket, silently promising to read it when I could. Right now, I needed to focus on survival. The church still held secrets – passages and hideaways the women's network had maintained since the war. Michelle had shown me most of them, and Thomas had clearly used at least one to escape with his sisters.

Morton's men were closing in. Soon, this house of God would become a battlefield.
Again.

"Spread out," Morton ordered quietly. "He's in there somewhere."

I moved silently toward the priest's chamber where I knew one of the escape tunnels began. But a voice stopped me – one I hadn't expected to hear.

"Allow me, Mr. Morton." Deacon Thompson's familiar tones carried clearly in the morning air. "I know how to talk to our wayward shepherd."

Heavy boots on wooden steps. Then Thompson's voice echoed through the empty church. "Victor? We need to talk, son."

The familial term, used so often in church meetings and prayer circles, now dripped with false concern. I stayed silent, watching from shadows as his shape filled the doorway.

"Twenty years is a long time," Thompson continued, moving inside. "Long time to watch a man play at being something he's not. Must have been hard, pretending to be a man of God when we both know what you really are." His footsteps moved closer to the altar. In the dim light, I could see he held no weapon – a calculated show of confidence that made him more dangerous, not less.

"Did Michelle know?" he asked conversationally. "About your real past? The women who went missing after your revivals in Louisiana? The convenient deaths that always seemed to follow your preaching?"
Ice formed in my veins. No one knew about that time – about the identity I'd taken from a dead man in Little Rock. No one except…

"She knew," Thompson said, reading my silence. "Found out months ago when she started digging into Morton's past. Found your real history too. Why do you think she prepared all these escape routes? These hidden supplies?" His voice turned gentle, mocking. "She wasn't preparing to run from Morton, Victor. She was preparing to run from you."

"Lies," I whispered, but doubt crept in like morning fog. "Is it? Ask yourself – why did she keep so many secrets? Why maintain this network of safe houses? Why keep that list of names?" He moved closer to where I hid. "The list you found in her Bible. The one you think proves her suspicions about me. Did you ever consider she was tracking your victims' families?

The people who might expose your true nature?"
"Stop it." My voice shook.
"Your own wife was gathering evidence against you,
Victor. Or whatever your real name is. She was going to
expose you, save your children from—"

My shot caught him high in the chest, the sound deafening
in the sacred space. Thompson staggered but didn't fall,
blood blooming across his Sunday best.
"Lies," I said again, stepping into view. "All of it lies."
He laughed, blood staining his teeth. "Are you sure? Check
the Henderson store. Not just the cellar – the hidden room
behind it. See what your precious Michelle really knew."
My second shot silenced him forever.

I stood in that sacred place, surrounded by death and
doubt. Thompson's words had planted seeds I couldn't
uproot. Michelle's secrets, her preparations, her silences…
But movement outside snapped me back to the present.
Morton's men were closing in. I'd taken too long, let
Thompson distract me with poisoned words.

A glint of metal caught my eye – there, scratched hastily on
the altar rail, three crosses. Thomas's signal that they were
safe but being followed. Below it, a series of marks
indicating they'd found shelter with friends.

My son's message cleared my mind like a dash of cold
water. Thompson's lies couldn't touch the truth I knew in
my bones. Michelle had been gathering evidence, yes – but
against Morton's conspiracy, not me. The preparations had
been to protect our children, not expose me.

I moved quickly to the hidden compartment behind the altar, gathering what supplies I could. But before I could reach the passage that would lead me to safety, Morton's voice rang out.

"Burn it," he ordered. "Burn it all."

The first flames licked at the church walls as Morton's men spread oil and set torches to ancient wood. Smoke began to fill the sanctuary, thick and choking. They meant to smoke me out or watch me burn.

I looked up at the cross still hanging above the altar, remembered all the sermons I'd preached about turning the other cheek. About forgiveness. About leaving vengeance to the Lord.

"Sorry, Lord," I whispered. "But sometimes the shepherd needs to become the wolf."

Checking my weapons one last time, I moved toward the priest's chamber. The old escape tunnel would take me behind their lines, give me the advantage of surprise. As smoke filled God's house, I thought of Thomas fighting here, protecting his sisters. Of Michelle maintaining these sanctuaries all these years, preparing for a day she prayed would never come.

Thompson had been right about one thing – twenty years was a long time to pretend to be something you're not. I wasn't pretending to be a killer anymore.

The church burned behind me as I moved through the woods, smoke rising like incense to an angry God. Thompson's last words echoed in my head, mixing with the stories I'd heard whispered about my past over the years. People love a good redemption story, but they love a hidden sin even more.

I'd never hidden what I was before finding Christ. Three years riding as a gun hand, taking any job that paid, building a reputation as a fast draw and a sure shot. Sixteen to nineteen, those were my lost years, my wandering in the wilderness. Until that revival in Louisiana where God found me and called me to a different kind of service.

But Thompson had twisted that truth into something darker. In his version, whispered to frightened townspeople, I'd been more than a hired gun. In his stories, I was a predator who used revivals to find victims, who left a trail of missing women and convenient deaths across three states. He'd taken my true past and corrupted it, like Satan twisting scripture in the wilderness.

The sound of horses brought me back to the present. Through the trees, I spotted Billy Henderson talking with two of Morton's men. The boy I'd watched grow up, who'd sat in my Sunday School, now stood with my family's killers.

"Check the north trail," one of Morton's men ordered. "Thompson said the preacher knows these woods too well to run blind."

"What about his kids?" the other asked. "That boy of his is smarter than we figured. Already killed Jenkins."

"Morton wants them alive," Billy said, his voice shaking. "Says they're evidence of the preacher's crimes."

I moved closer, staying in shadow. Billy's face was pale, his hands trembling on his rifle

. This was no willing conspirator – this was a frightened boy caught in Thompson's web.

"Don't see why we can't just kill 'em all," the first man grumbled. "Cleaner that way."

"Because Morton needs witnesses," the second replied. "Needs to prove Wright killed his first family back in Texas, that he's been killing folks at revivals for years. Thompson's got papers, testimonies from folks who lost kin at Wright's meetings." "All lies," Billy said quietly, then flinched as both men turned to him.

"What was that, boy?"

"I… I've seen Reverend Wright's past," Billy stammered. "In the papers Thompson keeps. He was a gunslinger, sure, but he changed. Got saved at nineteen. The rest… the missing women, the murders… Thompson made all that up."

The first man backhanded Billy, sending him sprawling. "Careful, boy. Sounds like you're having doubts about our righteous cause."

I'd heard enough. Two quick shots, and Morton's men lay dead. Billy scrambled backward, eyes wide with terror. "Please," he whimpered as I emerged from the trees. "They made me help them. Thompson said he'd take the store, send Ma to debtor's prison…
"

"Start at the beginning," I suggested, keeping my voice calm though my trigger finger itched. "What papers?"

"In… in the store. Hidden room behind the cellar wall. Thompson's been collecting things for months. Your real history as a gunslinger, but he changed it. Added false testimonies, fake witnesses. Made it look like you'd been killing folks at revivals for years." Billy's words tumbled out like spring flood. "But Miss Michelle… she found out what he was doing. Started gathering her own evidence."
"What evidence?"

"About Morton. About Thompson. She found proof they'd done this before – found other families with property they wanted, created false histories to destroy them. She was building a case against them, not you!" Relief flooded through me, washing away Thompson's poisoned doubts. Of course Michelle had been investigating – not to expose me, but to protect our family from Morton's conspiracy.

"Sir," Billy continued, tears running down his face, "I'm so sorry. When I heard what they did to Miss Michelle and the children…"

"Some of them lived," I reminded him. "Thanks to your silence, Morton nearly caught them. Still might."
"I know where they're headed!" Billy blurted.

"Thompson… he said Morton's got a place outside Little Rock. Old plantation called Willow Grove. That's where they're herding your kids – trying to drive them right into Morton's hands."

Another piece clicked into place. But before I could question Billy further, gunfire erupted from the burning church. Morton's men had found the tunnel.

"Go home," I told Billy. "Get your mother somewhere safe. When this is over, if I'm still alive, we'll talk about redemption."

He stared at me for a moment, then nodded and disappeared into the trees.

I moved quickly through the underbrush, working my way around to where Morton's remaining men gathered. Their voices carried clearly in the morning air.

"Spread out! Thompson said he'd be heading for the creek!"

"What about the Henderson boy?"

"Forget him. Morton wants the preacher. Says it's time to finish what started twenty years ago."

I smiled grimly in the shadows. Yes, it was time to finish this. But not the way Morton planned. I might have left my gunslinger past behind when I found God, but I hadn't forgotten its lessons.

Sometimes, to protect the flock, the shepherd needs to remember how to be a wolf.

The morning sun broke through the smoke as I tracked Morton's men through the woods. My old skills, buried under twenty years of scripture and sermons, rose to the surface like muscle memory. The gun in my hand felt familiar – not like the weapon it was, but like a tool for God's justice.

"You've lost your touch, preacher!" Morton's voice carried through the trees. "Time was you could outshoot any man from Texas to Tennessee. Now you're hiding like a scared rabbit!"

He was trying to goad me, using the fragments of truth he knew about my past. But I wasn't that hot-headed teenager anymore, quick to draw and quicker to shoot. Those three years as a gun hand had taught me patience as much as accuracy.

"Tell me something, James," I called back, moving silently through the underbrush. "How long did it take Thompson to find out about my gunslinger days? Must have been disappointed to learn I wasn't the cold-blooded killer you needed for your story."

"Disappointed?" Morton laughed, but there was an edge to it. "Boy, we built a better story than anything your real past could give us. Seventeen women gone missing after your revivals. Three families murdered in their beds. Even a dead preacher in Louisiana whose identity you stole."
"All lies," I said, positioning myself behind a massive oak. "Except the last part. But you got that wrong too."
"Did we?" Morton's voice was closer now. "The real Victor Wright died in Louisiana. You took his name, his calling. Tell me I'm wrong."

"The real Victor Wright was my father," I said quietly, knowing he could hear me. "He died bringing God's word to lost souls, and I took up his mantle. Nothing hidden, nothing stolen. Just a son honoring his father's legacy."

A shot splintered bark near my head. Morton's patience was wearing thin.

"Pretty story," he spat. "But it won't matter what's true once Thompson's evidence is presented in court. Your children will testify against you. The whole county will learn what kind of monster's been preaching to them all these years."

I stayed silent, letting him talk. Every word helped me track his position.

"You know what's funny?" Morton continued, moving steadily closer to where I waited. "Thompson really believed it. All those false witnesses we paid, all those fake testimonies – he convinced himself they were real. Started seeing you as some kind of devil in preacher's clothes. Even had Michelle believing it at the end."

My trigger finger tightened, but I forced myself to wait.

"You're lying about my wife."

"Am I? Why do you think she kept all those files? All that evidence? She was planning to expose you, save her children from—"

My shot cut him off, the bullet grazing his shoulder and spinning him around. Before his men could react, I put a second round through his gun hand.

"Michelle kept files on you," I said, stepping into view. "On Thompson. On your whole conspiracy. Twenty years of evidence about your real business – finding properties you wanted, destroying families to get them, using false histories to cover your crimes."

Morton's face went pale, either from blood loss or from truth. His remaining men had their guns trained on me, but uncertainty showed in their stance.

"You two-bit gunslinger," Morton snarled. "You don't know anything!"

"I know Thompson was your brother-in-law, not your friend. I know he helped you pick targets – families with property you wanted, women you could manipulate. I know Michelle figured it all out months ago and started building a case against you both."

"Lies!"

"Then why did Thompson keep secrets from you? Why didn't he show you what was in that hidden room at the Henderson store? He was playing both sides, James. Building a case to destroy us both."

One of Morton's men lowered his gun slightly. "Boss? What's he talking about?"

"Shoot him!" Morton screamed. "Shoot him now!"

But I was already moving. Three shots rang out almost as one – two men fell, and Morton took another round in his shoulder.

"Twenty years," I said, standing over him as he bled into Arkansas soil. "Twenty years you watched my family, planned their destruction. And in the end, you were just Thompson's pawn."

"Kill me then," he spat. "Prove you're the killer they say you are."

I looked at him – this man who'd murdered my family, who'd twisted my past into a monster's tale, who'd tried to destroy everything I'd built. The gunslinger in me wanted to end him right there.

But I wasn't just a gunslinger anymore. "No," I said finally. "I'm not going to kill you." Hope flickered in his eyes. "I'm going to let you live," I continued. "Live long enough to face justice. To watch as Michelle's evidence exposes your true past. To see everything you built collapse around you."

I knelt beside him, letting him see what his actions had turned me into – not the killer he'd invented, but something perhaps more dangerous: a righteous man with nothing left to lose.

"But first, you're going to tell me everything about Thompson's plan. About where my children might be. And James?" I pressed my gun under his chin. "You better pray they're still alive."

The sun climbed higher as Morton talked, spilling secrets like blood into the morning air. With each word, the true scope of Thompson's betrayal became clear – and with it, the knowledge that my greatest battle still lay ahead. Morton's confession poured out between gasps of pain, each word revealing a conspiracy deeper than I'd imagined. Thompson had been the architect of it all, using his position as deacon to identify vulnerable families across three states

. Morton was just his latest tool – a blunt instrument aimed at families with property Thompson coveted.

"Your wife," Morton wheezed, "she figured it out first. Started connecting the pieces after Thompson bought the bank. Saw the pattern of foreclosures, mysterious deaths, families driven out…"

"Keep talking." I pressed the gun harder under his chin. "Thompson… he's got a judge in his pocket. Papers ready to declare you unfit, give him guardianship of your surviving children. Then the property transfers to him, legal and clean."

"And you? What was your cut supposed to be?" Morton laughed, a wet sound full of blood. "Cut? I was just the fall guy. Thompson planned to pin everything on me once you were gone. Had papers ready to prove I acted alone, killed your family against his wishes."

Understanding dawned cold and clear. "That's why he kept secrets from you. Why he didn't share everything Michelle discovered."

"Stupid old man actually believes the stories he made up about you. Convinced himself you're some kind of devil. But me?" Morton coughed, spitting blood. "I just wanted Michelle back. Everything else was Thompson's plan."

"Where are they meeting? My children – where's Thompson taking them?"

"Willow Grove plantation. But…" Morton's eyes rolled wildly. "You don't understand.

Thompson's not trying to catch them. He's herding them there for a reason. Your boy Thomas… he's got

something Thompson wants. Something Michelle gave him…"
"What? What did she give him?"
But Morton's eyes were glazing over, consciousness fading. I grabbed his shirt front, shook him hard.
"Stay with me, James. What did Michelle give Thomas?"
"Book," he mumbled. "Little black book. Names, dates… everything Thompson's done for thirty years. Michelle… she found his records… gave them to Thomas…"
The pieces clicked together. Michelle hadn't just been gathering evidence – she'd found Thompson's own records, his documentation of decades of crimes.

She'd given them to Thomas for safekeeping, knowing he was the most careful of our children.
"Thompson knows?" I demanded.
Morton nodded weakly. "Why he wants them alive. Needs… needs that book… Can't let anyone see…"
"How many men at Willow Grove?"
"Doesn't matter," Morton's voice was fading.
"Thompson… he's not what you think. Not just some corrupt deacon. He was… was something else before.

During the war…" "What? What was he?"
But Morton's head lolled back, unconscious or dead – I didn't stop to check which. The sun was high now, and my children were being driven toward a trap laid by a man more dangerous than I'd realized.

I searched Morton's pockets, finding letters, maps, and finally a small leather diary. Its pages confirmed everything – Thompson's plans, his network of corrupt officials, his decades of crimes. But it was the last entry that chilled my blood:

"Wright children must not reach Little Rock. If judge sees evidence M. gave them, everything falls apart. Better they die in escape attempt. Cleaner that way."

My hands shook as I read the words. Thompson wasn't trying to capture my children – he was planning to murder them and claim they died trying to flee. Just another tragedy to pin on their "murderous" father.

I took what supplies I could from Morton and his men, including fresh ammunition and a better rifle. The maps showed Willow Grove was half a day's ride, but I knew these woods better than Thompson. There were old trails, paths from before the war, that could get me there faster. As I mounted up, movement caught my eye. Billy Henderson stepped out of the trees, his young face set with determination.

"I'm coming with you," he said before I could speak. "I know Willow Grove. My pa used to work there before… before Thompson took it from him."

I studied him carefully. The boy I'd watched grow up was gone, replaced by a man ready to face hard truths. "Thompson killed my pa," Billy continued. "Made it look like an accident when he couldn't pay his loans. I was too young to understand then, but now…" He straightened his shoulders. "I need to make this right."

I thought of Michelle's teachings about redemption, about how it's never too late to choose the right path. After a moment, I nodded.

"Mount up," I said. "But understand this – what happens at Willow Grove won't be pretty. Thompson's not just trying to catch my children. He means to kill them."

"I know," Billy replied, swinging into his saddle. "Miss Michelle… she trusted me once. Told me to watch out for the little ones if anything happened. I failed her then. I won't fail again."

We rode hard through the heat of the day, following tracks only a father's eyes could see. Thomas was leading his sisters well, but I could tell they were tiring. The signs of their passage showed increasing fatigue – dragging feet, more frequent rests.

And behind their trail, other signs. Thompson's men, herding them steadily toward Willow Grove.
Toward what waited in that old plantation house.
Willow Grove rose from the evening mist like a monster awakening. The old plantation house stood dark against the bloodred sunset, its white columns stained gray with age and darker sins. Spanish moss hung from ancient willows like funeral shrouds, stirring in a wind that carried the scent of coming rain.

Billy and I crouched at the edge of the tree line, watching Thompson's men patrol the grounds. Their movements were too precise for hired guns – more like soldiers keeping watch. Four men on the ground level, two more visible through upstairs windows, all of them armed with military rifles.

"More guards than usual," Billy whispered, his young face grave in the fading light.

"Thompson's expecting trouble."

"Tell me about that cellar entrance again."

Billy sketched a rough map in the dirt with a stick.

"Loading dock's round back, hidden by old cargo boxes.

Door's heavy – iron, not wood. Pa found it when he was investigating Thompson. Before the 'accident.'"

I studied the patrol patterns, timing their movements.

"Your father... what exactly did he find down there?"

"Records at first. Ledgers showing Thompson's schemes. But then..." Billy's voice caught. "There were other things. Medical equipment from the war. Journals about experiments

. Pa said Thompson wasn't just a doctor back then – he was something else. Something that didn't stop when the war did."

A scream cut through the evening air – high and terrified. Grace's voice. My youngest daughter, who'd never raised her voice in anger, was screaming in pure terror.

Every fiber of my being wanted to charge the house, guns blazing. The old gunslinger in me knew I could take down half of them before they knew what hit them. But that would get my children killed.

"How many ways into the main house from the cellar?" I forced myself to focus, to think past the rage.

"Two. Servant's stairs come up in the kitchen, and there's a hidden door in the old parlor. Pa used that one to…" Billy stopped as Grace screamed again.

"Listen carefully," I said, checking my weapons. "I need you to create a distraction. Something big enough to draw their attention away from the cellar entrance.

Can you do that?"

Billy nodded, his face set with determination. "Yes sir. I brought some of Pa's old dynamite. Been saving it for something that mattered."

"Your father would be proud, son." I touched his shoulder briefly. "Set it on the far side of the house. Wait for my signal – three shots, close together. Then run. Don't try to be a hero."

"What about you?"

I thought of Michelle, of our lost children, of twenty years of lies and betrayal. "I'm going to show Thompson what happens when wolves threaten a shepherd's lambs."

We separated, moving through deepening shadows. The sun was almost gone now, painting the world in shades of blood and darkness. As I approached the loading dock, another scream echoed from above – Rachel this time, calling her sister's name.

The cellar door was just as Billy described, iron-bound and heavy. But the lock was old, susceptible to the tools Michelle's friends had provided in our last sanctuary. As I worked the mechanism, voices drifted down from above.

"Brave little lambs," Thompson's voice, carrying that familiar false kindness
. "Just like your mother. She was brave too, right up until the end. Now, Thomas, about that book your mother gave you…" The lock clicked open.

I checked my guns one last time, touched Michelle's Bible in my pocket. The cellar steps descended into darkness that stank of old death and older sins. Even after decades, the air carried memories of Thompson's war work – a medicinal smell that couldn't quite mask something worse beneath.

Whatever Thompson had been during the war, whatever dark purpose had driven him since, ended tonight. Time to show him what a father's love could do.
Time to remind him that even Jesus used a whip when evil men defiled his Father's house.

The cellar steps creaked softly under my weight despite my care. In the darkness, my foot struck something that rolled away with a hollow sound. A shaft of light from above revealed what I already knew – a human skull, yellowed with age. Billy had been right. This place held darker secrets than mere corruption.

"Your father's coming, you know." Thompson's voice drifted down clearer now. "Coming to see what his sins have wrought. Did he ever tell you about his gunslinger days? About the men he killed before he found his… calling?"

"Our father's a good man." Thomas's voice, steady despite what must be fear. My boy, so much like his mother. "Better than you'll ever be."

A sharp crack – the sound of a hand striking flesh – then Rachel's angry cry: "Don't you touch him!"
"Such spirit," Thompson mocked. "Your mother had spirit too. Right up until she realized what your father really was. Why do you think she kept all those files? All those records?"

"To expose you," Thomas shot back. "She found proof of what you did during the war. What you've been doing since."

Another crack, another blow. I moved faster through the darkness, following the voices toward the hidden door Billy had described.

"The war?" Thompson laughed, but there was an edge of madness in it. "I've seen things in war that would shatter your innocent minds. Done things that would make your father's sins look like child's play. I wasn't just a doctor, boy. I was an artist. A creator. Those men, those experiments… I was making them better."

"You're insane," Thomas said quietly.
"Insane? I've spent twenty years building a perfect life here. Respected deacon, trusted friend, pillar of the community. While your father played at redemption, I was perfecting my art. And now…" A pause. "Now you'll give me that book your mother entrusted to you, or I'll show you exactly what I learned in those field hospitals."

"Don't, Thomas!" Grace's voice, strong despite her fear. "Mama said we had to keep it safe!"

I reached the hidden door, found the mechanism Billy had described. Through gaps in the paneling, I could see into the parlor. Thompson stood by the fireplace, still wearing his bloodstained church clothes. Thomas sat bound to a straight-backed chair, face bruised but eyes defiant. Grace and Rachel huddled together on a settee, tear-stained but unbroken. Four armed men stood watch, their weapons held with military precision.

"Brave little lamb," Thompson said to Grace, moving toward her with that familiar pastoral smile. "Just like your mother. She was brave too, right up until—"

"Until what?" I stepped through the hidden door, both guns drawn. "Until you had Morton murder her while I was away? While you made sure no help would come?" The room froze. Thompson recovered first, his smile never wavering. "Victor. I was just telling your children about their father's colorful past. About the killer who hid behind a collar, who murdered his way across three states." "The only killer here is you." I moved further into the room, keeping my children behind me. "You're not just a corrupt deacon or a crooked businessman.

You're something that should have died in the war." "The war?" Thompson's smile turned cruel. "The war showed me what men really are. What they can become with the right... improvements. Your children have so much potential, Victor. Just like those soldiers in my hospital. So much room for... enhancement."

The madness in his eyes was clear now, the mask of respectability finally falling away.

This was what Billy's father had discovered, what Michelle had found in those hidden records. Thompson hadn't just been a doctor during the war – he'd been a monster wearing a doctor's coat.

"You're wrong about one thing," I said calmly. "I never hid what I was. Three years as a gun hand, taking any job that paid. But God found me at nineteen, gave me a new purpose. My father's name, his calling – I took them up honestly, openly."

"Pretty story," Thompson sneered. "But I've spent twenty years building a better one. And once your children have their tragic accident trying to escape their murderous father…"

The world exploded into chaos as Billy's dynamite rocked the far side of the house. Thompson's men turned instinctively toward the sound – a fatal mistake. I dropped two before they could turn back. A third got off a wild shot that splintered the chair where Thomas had been, but my son was already rolling free, the ropes somehow cut. The fourth man had time to aim, but Rachel was her mother's daughter – the heavy vase she threw spoiled his shot perfectly.

Thompson himself drew a hidden gun, but Grace – my brave, tiny Grace – threw herself at his legs. As he stumbled, Thomas tackled him fully, wrestling something from his coat – the little black book Michelle had entrusted to him.

"Run!" I ordered, laying down covering fire as Billy appeared at the back door, rifle ready. "Get to the horses!"

"You can't leave," Thompson called, rising despite his wounds, madness now fully unveiled. "Don't you want to know what else I can make you? What improvements—"

The explosion that followed – whether from Billy's remaining dynamite or God's own judgment – cut him off. Flames engulfed the parlor as we fled, consuming Thompson and his house of horrors.

We rode hard through the night, my children pressed close, heading for the safety of Little Rock. Behind us, Willow Grove burned against the sky like God's own vengeance.

But we carried truth with us – Thompson's records in that little black book, proof of decades of evil done in shadow. There would be justice, in time.

"Papa," Grace whispered as we rode, her small arms tight around my waist. "Are we safe now?"

I thought of Morton, still out there somewhere. Of Thompson's network of corrupt officials. Of the long road ahead.

"Not yet, little one," I said honestly. "But we're together. And your mama taught me that's where safety truly begins."

The moon rose as we rode, bright and clean after the smoke and darkness. We had lost so much – my beloved Michelle, our home, seven precious souls that no earthly justice could restore. But we had gained something too:

truth, purpose, and the knowledge that sometimes a shepherd must become a wolf to protect what remains of his flock.

Dawn would find us closer to justice, closer to peace. But first, James Morton waited to learn what happened when a father's love met a killer's justice.

CHAPTER 5:

The Shepherds Allies

(Watkins Manor Front View)

(Watkins Manor Rear View)-(Courtyard)

The first bullet I never felt. Might have been the rush of escape, the pounding of hooves, or simply God's mercy that kept the pain at bay. We'd ridden hard through the night after Willow Grove burned, my children pressed close, the evidence of Thompson's evil secure in Thomas's saddlebag.

It was Rachel who noticed first. My observant ten-year-old, always watching, always aware – just like her mama.
"Papa," her voice drifted up from what seemed a great distance. "Papa, you're bleeding!"
The world had started spinning by then, the morning sun dancing strangely in the sky. We'd stopped at a watering hole, the horses drinking deep, when the first wave of dizziness hit me.

"Thomas," I managed, seeing two of my oldest son as he turned toward me. "Take your sisters… Little Rock… Michelle's friend…"

Then the ground rose up to meet me, and darkness took everything away.

Voices drifted through the darkness over what seemed years:

"…fever's awful high…"

"…gonna lose the leg if we don't…"

"…Papa, please wake up…"

"…just like I told you, child – your daddy's too damn stubborn to die…"

I woke to the sound of children's laughter – my children's laughter – floating through an open window. For a moment, I thought I was home, that the past weeks had been nothing but a nightmare. But this room… this room was like nothing I'd ever seen. Sunlight streamed through floor-to-ceiling windows draped with silk that probably cost more than my entire farm.

The bed beneath me was massive, carved from mahogany and covered in the finest linens. A crystal chandelier hung from an ornately plastered ceiling, and the furniture looked like it had come straight from some European palace. "Well, well! Sleeping Beauty finally decides to join the land of the living!"

The voice boomed like thunder, and for a moment I thought the whole mansion shook. I turned my head to see what had to be the biggest man I'd ever laid eyes on filling the doorway – and I mean filling it. He had to turn sideways and duck just to enter the room, his fine purple silk vest and gold watch chain making him look like a well-dressed mountain come to life.

"Name's Lawrence Watkins," he announced, his massive frame settling into a groaning chair beside my bed. "But folks round here just call me Big Daddy. Course, looking at me, ain't hard to figure why!"

His laugh was as big as he was, rolling through the room like summer storm. Standing, he had to be six foot nine if he was an inch, and well over five hundred pounds. His gray hair and beard were wild as mountain sage, but his eyes twinkled with intelligence and humor. Despite his size, he moved with the easy grace of a man used to commanding respect – and getting it.

"Your young'uns been wearing me out for two weeks now," he continued, grinning through his beard. "That Rachel of yours, she's got more questions than a seminary student on examination day. And Thomas – boy's already better with horses than half my hands. Course, little Grace…" His voice softened. "That one's got the gift. Saw her heal one of my dogs yesterday just by singing to it."

My throat was dry as dust, but I managed to croak out, "Two weeks?"

"Fourteen days, four hours, and…" he pulled out a massive pocket watch that looked tiny in his ham-sized hands, "…thirty-seven minutes since your children dragged your bleeding carcass onto my property.

Lucky for you, old Doc Matthews was visiting. He's the best sawbones in three states, when he's sober enough to see straight."

He gestured around the opulent room. "Built all this myself, you know. Started with one cotton field after the war, now got me twenty thousand acres, three cotton mills, and the finest horse breeding operation in four states. Man can do a lot when he puts his mind to it.

His massive frame shifted in the groaning chair, those intelligent eyes studying me carefully. "Course, your children also told me quite a story about how you all ended up bleeding on my property. Quite a tale indeed." He paused, stroking his wild beard. "Funny thing is, I heard a different version of that story bout twenty years back. Bout a preacher who stole another man's wife in Texas. Man named Morton, if I recall."

My hand instinctively moved toward where my gun should be, but Big Daddy's booming laugh filled the room. "Now, now, don't get yourself worked up. I learned long ago there's usually more than one side to any story. And having spent two weeks with your children…" He shook his head in admiration. "Well, let's just say any man who could raise young'uns with that much grace and strength ain't the villain Morton made you out to be."

Through the open door, I could see Rachel passing in the hallway, her arms full of law books nearly as big as she was. Thomas's voice drifted up from somewhere below, discussing cattle prices with what sounded like experienced traders.

"They've taken to this place like ducks to water," Big Daddy said proudly. "Thomas especially. Boy's got a mind for business I ain't seen in years. Been helping me review contracts, spotting things my own lawyers missed." His expression grew serious. "But we need to talk about your situation, Reverend Wright."

Before I could respond, footsteps thundered up the stairs, a sound from the doorway caught my attention. My breath caught in my throat – there stood my three surviving children, looking cleaner and better dressed than I'd ever seen them. Thomas had grown an inch, it seemed, in just two weeks. Rachel's hair was neatly braided, and Grace… my baby girl's face lit up like sunshine breaking through storm clouds.

"Papa!" Grace started to run forward but caught herself, remembering her manners even in her excitement. The other two showed similar restraint, though I could see how much they wanted to rush to my side.

"Oh, go on," Big Daddy's laugh boomed like thunder. "Proper manners can wait when a man's been sleeping for two weeks."

The next moments were a blur of embraces, tears, and jumbled words of love and relief.
My children were alive, were safe. In that moment, nothing else mattered.

"Alright now," Big Daddy's voice softened, if something that massive could truly be soft. "Let your papa breathe. Sally's got fresh biscuits downstairs, and I need a word with your father."

The children reluctantly pulled away, each touching me one last time as if to make sure I was real. Thomas, looking more man than boy now, helped Grace down from the bed.

"We'll be back soon, Papa," Rachel promised, her eyes bright with unshed tears. "Mrs. Sally's been teaching us proper manners for dinner. Wait till you see the dining room – it's bigger than our whole church!"

After they left, Big Daddy settled back in his groaning chair. "Fine children," he said thoughtfully. "Don't make 'em like that much anymore.

Most young ones these days, give 'em a house like this and they turn wild as March hares. Yours though…" He shook his massive head. "Been helping with the horses, minding their studies, even handling the house slaves with proper respect. Your Michelle raised them right." The mention of my wife's name sent a sharp pain through my chest.

"Ah yes, Michelle," Big Daddy's booming voice softened with the memory. "You probably don't remember meeting my Martha and me. Must've been, oh, ten years back at that revival you held just outside Memphis. Middle of July it was – hot as Satan's kitchen."

He shifted in his chair, which protested under his enormous weight. "Martha had been feeling poorly, and the doctors in Little Rock couldn't figure what ailed her. We'd heard tell of a preacher with a healing touch, so we came to see for ourselves." His massive frame shook with a gentle laugh. "Course, being the size I am, we had to sit way in the back. Couldn't fit these shoulders between them skinny pews."

A distant look came into his eyes. "Your Michelle spotted us right away – came straight back with a pitcher of lemonade and some cornbread. Said no one should suffer through a Tennessee summer without proper refreshment. Had little Thomas with her, couldn't have been more than three at the time.

Most peculiar thing…" He leaned forward, making the chair groan ominously. "My prized stallion had gone lame that morning – mean creature that wouldn't let anyone near him. Found your boy out in the stable tent, sitting right next to that horse, feeding him apple slices like they were old friends."

"The revival outside Memphis," I said slowly, the memory starting to form. "That was you? The plantation owner whose wife was suffering from…"

"The wasting disease, yes," Big Daddy nodded. "Doctors said Martha had six months at best. But your Michelle…" He shook his head in wonder. "She took one look at my wife and said it wasn't her time yet.

Spent the whole afternoon with us after the service, talking and praying. Sent us home with a jar of some herbal tonic she'd made. Martha lived another five blessed years after that."

He pulled out his pocket watch, massive fingers surprisingly gentle as he opened it to reveal a small portrait. "That's my Martha there. Picture was taken the day after your revival. First time she'd felt strong enough to sit for a portrait in months. She never forgot your family's kindness. Used to say there was something special about your Michelle, something in her eyes that could see right through to a person's soul."

"I remember now," I said. "Michelle talked about you both for weeks after. Said she'd never met a man big as a bear with a heart soft as butter."

Big Daddy's laugh boomed through the room. "That sounds like her alright. Sharp eyes, that woman had. Maybe too sharp for her own good." His face grew serious. "That's probably why Thompson wanted her gone. Man like that, with secrets that dark, wouldn't want someone around who could see the truth in him."

Big Daddy's expression shifted from reminiscence to something more serious. His massive frame leaned forward, making the chair protest beneath him.
"Now then, Reverend, let's talk about your situation." He pulled out another cigar the size of a small log. "Your children have told me everything while you've been healing up.

About Thompson, about Morton, about what happened to your Michelle and the little ones."

He lit the cigar, the flame catching in his serious eyes. "Way I figure it, you got three problems. First, you got Morton still out there somewhere, nursing two bullet wounds and a grudge. Second, you got Thompson's friends in high places – judges, bankers, men who'll want that book your wife found.

And third…" He exhaled a cloud of smoke. "You got nowhere to go and no resources to fight with."

A smile spread beneath his wild beard. "Lucky for you, I got solutions to all three." "I can't ask you to—" I started, but his massive hand waved away my protest.

"Ain't asking, Reverend. I owe your Michelle for the five extra years I got with my Martha. Besides," his eyes twinkled, "ain't often a man my size gets to play David against Goliath."

He stood, moving to the window despite his bulk. "First off, you and your children are staying here as long as needed. Got two hundred rooms in this place – might as well put some to good use. Thomas can help with my horses – boy's got a gift I ain't seen since… well, since my own son. Rachel's already reorganizing my library, and little Grace…" He chuckled. "Cook says she's never seen biscuits rise so high."

"As for Morton," he continued, "I got men watching every road between here and Texas. Best trackers in three states. He shows his face anywhere near here, we'll know. And them friends of Thompson's?" His laugh shook the windows. "Let's just say I got some friends of my own. Powerful men who don't take kindly to folk who hurt children."

He turned back to me, his jovial face suddenly serious. "But most important, I got something you're gonna need – proof. Evidence that goes back to the war, showing what Thompson and his kind were really doing. Add that to your wife's book…" He spread his massive hands. "Well, let's just say some very important people are gonna have some very uncomfortable questions to answer."

"Why would you do all this?" I asked. "You barely know us."

"Three reasons," he held up thick fingers. "First, like I said, I owe your Michelle. Second, I got my own score to settle with Thompson's crowd from the war. And third…" His voice softened. "Watching your Thomas with them horses, seeing little Grace's smile… reminds me of my boy. What he could've been, if I'd been smart enough, brave enough to stop Thompson back then."

He settled back in his groaning chair.

"So here's what we're gonna do…"

"Lawrence Watkins!" Sally's voice cut through the room like a steel blade. "What did I tell you about exciting my patient?"

Big Daddy's massive frame actually flinched as the dignified Black woman swept into the room, followed by a weathered-looking man with twinkling eyes who could only be Doc Matthews.

"Now Sally," Big Daddy started, but she cut him off with a look that could have wilted an oak tree.

"Don't you 'Now Sally' me. I've been changing your diapers since before you could walk, and size ain't never stopped me from taking you to task." She turned to Doc Matthews. "Can you believe this man?

Patient's barely awake and he's in here plotting and planning like it's a war council."

Doc Matthews grinned, setting down his medical bag. "Well, considering our friend here survived a bullet that should've killed him, rode half dead for miles, and then slept for two weeks… I'd say he's earned the right to plot a little." He winked at me. "Though I got to admit, Reverend, you're either the luckiest man alive or the most stubborn."

"Stubborn," Sally declared, shooing Big Daddy from his chair so she could check my bandages. "Just like someone else I know." She shot a meaningful look at Big Daddy. "Lord have mercy, woman," Big Daddy's laugh boomed. "You trying to compare me to this scrap of a preacher? I got at least three hundred pounds on him!"

"And about half the sense," Doc Matthews chuckled, checking my pulse. "Though I got to say, Lawrence, feeding him up the way Sally's been doing, he might catch up to you yet."

"Ha!" Big Daddy's belly shook. "The day this reverend reaches my size is the day I'll eat my own hat!"
"Don't tempt me," Sally muttered, making Doc Matthews snort with laughter. "I've still got all your old suits in storage. Could probably fit two of him in one leg."
I watched this exchange with growing amazement – this tiny woman ordering around a man who could have crushed her with one hand, a country doctor trading jokes with one of the wealthiest men in Arkansas, all of them acting like family despite their differences.

"Now then," Doc Matthews said, finishing his examination. "Wound's healing clean, fever's gone. Sally's cooking's put some meat back on your bones. I'd say our reverend friend here is going to make it." He grinned. "Though if he's smart, he'll listen to Sally better than some other patients I could name."

"Speaking of which," Sally fixed Big Daddy with another stern look. "Ain't you got some business to attend to? Something that don't involve tiring out my patient?"
"Yes ma'am," Big Daddy said meekly, though his eyes twinkled. "Though you might want to tell Doc here the same thing

. Man talks more than a church full of ladies after Sunday service."
"At least I ain't big enough to block out the sun when I stand up," Doc shot back good-naturedly.
"Both of you, out," Sally ordered, though there was fondness in her voice. "My patient needs rest, not a comedy show."

As they headed for the door, still trading friendly insults, Big Daddy turned back. "Rest up, Reverend. We'll finish our talk when Sally gives permission." He winked. "Which, knowing her, might be sometime next year."
"I heard that!" Sally called after him, making both men laugh as they left.

She turned back to me, her dignified face softening. "Don't you worry none about them. Big Daddy's heart's as large as he is, and Doc's the best physician in three states, even if he does talk too much." She adjusted my pillows with practiced ease

. "Now then, let's see about getting some real food in you. Can't have you wasting away in my care."

"That man," Sally shook her head as she straightened my blankets, "got a heart big as he is, but sometimes I swear he's still that same boy who used to sneak extra biscuits from my kitchen."

"You've known him that long?" I asked, watching her efficient movements.

"Since the day he was born. Was there when his mama passed, God rest her soul. Raised him best I could, though Lord knows it wasn't easy. Boy ate more than three grown men by the time he was twelve." Her stern face softened with memory. "Course, that was before the war changed everything."

Doc Matthews returned, carrying a steaming bowl. "Now Sally, don't go telling all the family secrets. Man's barely met us."

"Hush now," she took the bowl from him. "If he's staying under this roof, he needs to know what kind of circus he's walked into." She helped me sit up straighter. "This here's my special chicken soup.

Same recipe I used to feed Big Daddy when he was sick as a child. Never failed yet."

"That's because anyone too weak to run away has to eat it," Doc quipped, earning himself a stern look.

"I don't see you turning it down when you've had too much of your medicine," Sally shot back, making the doctor laugh.

"Guilty as charged." He settled into the chair Big Daddy had vacated, pulling out a flask. "Speaking of which…"

"Marcus Matthews, it ain't even noon yet!"

"Best time for it," he grinned, taking a sip. "Helps steady the hands for doctoring."

"Helps steady everything but your tongue," Sally muttered, but there was fondness in her voice.

As I sipped the soup – which was indeed remarkable – Doc Matthews leaned forward. "Now then, Reverend, since our large friend got interrupted, there's something you should know. That bullet wound wasn't just luck or bad aim. Someone knew exactly where to shoot to make you bleed slow but steady.

Military training, I'd say."

Sally's hands stilled in their work. "Doc…"

"He needs to know, Sally." The doctor's jovial manner faded. "Thompson wasn't working alone. During the war, he trained others in his… methods. Some of them are still out there. Still watching."

A shadow passed the window – one of Big Daddy's armed guards making their rounds.

"That's why Lawrence has this place guarded like a fortress," Doc continued. "After what happened to his boy… well, let's just say he's been preparing for something like this for a long time."

"Which is all he needs to know right now," Sally said firmly. "Man needs rest, not more worries."

"Just one more thing," Doc Matthews stood, suddenly serious. "That book your wife found – Big Daddy showed it to me. Some of those medical notes…" He shuddered. "I served as an army surgeon. Saw things that still give me nightmares. But what Thompson was doing… that wasn't medicine. That was something else entirely."

"And that's enough!" Sally's voice cracked like a whip. "Out with you now. Man can't heal with you filling his head with such talk."

Doc Matthews raised his hands in surrender, but paused at the door. "One last thing, Reverend. Your boy Thomas… keep him close. What he can do with horses – I've only seen that once before. In Big Daddy's son, just before Thompson took an interest in him."

After he left, Sally busied herself tidying the already immaculate room. "Don't you fret none about all that," she said softly. "Big Daddy may talk big, but he means what he says about protecting you and yours. Ain't seen him take to children like this since…" She stopped, emotion crossing her face. "Well, since his own boy." From somewhere below, I could hear Grace's voice raised in song, accompanied by Rachel's laugh and what sounded like Thomas talking to horses.

"Your children are safe here," Sally continued, her dignity returning. "This house has more secrets than a church has prayers. And Big Daddy…" She smiled. "Well, let's just say there's a reason even the governor thinks twice before crossing him."

Sally was adjusting my pillows when heavy boots sounded in the hallway. Big Daddy's massive frame filled the doorway again, but this time his jovial expression was replaced with something more serious.

"Sally," his voice was uncharacteristically quiet, "got a rider coming up the south road. One of Morton's men, by the description."

"Lawrence Watkins, don't you dare—"
"Now Sally," he raised one ham-sized hand, "ain't planning on doing nothing foolish.

Just thought our friend here might want to know what's happening under his own roof." He turned to me. "Seems Morton's offering rewards for information about you and your children. Got men spreading word in every town from here to Texas."

Sally's face hardened. "Let them come. Ain't the first time this house has kept secrets." "No, it ain't," Big Daddy agreed, then grinned suddenly. "Besides, might be interesting to see their faces when they realize whose hospitality they're testing."

Doc Matthews reappeared, slightly unsteady but eyes sharp. "Want me to have a word with our visitor, Lawrence? Being the county doctor, might seem natural for me to be treating a gunshot victim."

"No need," Big Daddy's grin widened. "Got something better in mind." He turned to Sally. "Where's Thomas?"
"Out in the south pasture with that wild stallion of yours. The one none of your men could…" She stopped,

understanding crossing her face. "Lawrence, you ain't thinking…"

"Think about it," his eyes twinkled. "Morton's man rides up, sees a boy doing what twenty grown men couldn't. Might make him think twice about who he's dealing with."

"Or might make him more determined to take the children," I managed to say, trying to rise.

"Now don't you start," Sally pushed me gently back. "Ain't nobody taking nothing from this house that Big Daddy don't want taken."

"She's right," Doc Matthews nodded. "You know what they called Lawrence during the war? The Mountain That Moves. Wasn't just cause of his size, neither."

Big Daddy shifted uncomfortably. "That was a long time ago, Marcus."

"Maybe," the doctor took another sip from his flask. "But I notice you still keep that old uniform locked up. The one with all them special pockets for…"

"That's enough," Sally cut in sharply. "Ain't no need to dig up old graves today."

A commotion rose from the courtyard below – horses whinnying, men shouting. We all moved to the window (Sally protesting but helping me stand). In the paddock below, Thomas stood calmly beside a massive black stallion, his hand resting easily on its neck. The horse, which had reportedly injured three stable hands last week, was docile as a lamb.

A stranger sat his horse at the fence, watching. Even from this distance, I could see the man's stunned expression.

"Watch this," Big Daddy murmured.

Thomas stepped away from the stallion, made a small gesture. The huge horse dropped to its knees, then rolled over like a trained dog. Another gesture, and it rose, shaking itself before nuzzling my son's shoulder.

"Sweet Jesus," Doc Matthews whispered. "Boy's even better than…"

"Than my Jacob was," Big Daddy finished quietly. "Now you see why we got to protect him? Why Thompson wanted…" He stopped as more hoofbeats approached. Two riders entered the courtyard, guns visible on their hips. Morton's men, by their bearing. They reined up hard at the sight of Thomas and the stallion.

"Time to give them something to think about," Big Daddy straightened to his full height. "Sally, help our friend back to bed. Doc, come with me. Let's go explain to these gentlemen exactly whose property they're trespassing on."

From my window, I watched Big Daddy stride into the courtyard, his massive frame making the armed riders look like children on ponies.

Despite his size, he moved with the fluid grace of a man who knew how to handle trouble.

"Afternoon, gentlemen," his voice boomed across the yard. "Seems you've wandered onto private property."

The first rider, a lean man with a scarred face, tried to look down at Big Daddy – a difficult feat even from horseback.

"Looking for a preacher and some kids. Heard tell they might be in these parts."

"That so?" Big Daddy pulled out one of his massive cigars, taking his time lighting it. "And who might be doing this telling?"

"Man named Morton," the second rider said. "Offering good money for information."

"James Morton?" Big Daddy's laugh shook the windows. "Now that's a name I ain't heard in a while." He took a long draw on his cigar. "Tell me something – he mention how he got them two bullet holes my friend put in him?" The riders' hands drifted toward their guns. "Your friend?" "Mhmm," Big Daddy nodded pleasantly, smoke curling around his huge frame.

"Reverend Wright's been a guest of mine since that unfortunate business at his home. Man's got a way with a gun that's downright biblical, if you take my meaning." "Then you're harboring a murderer," Scarface snarled, drawing his pistol.

What happened next moved almost too fast to follow. Despite his enormous size, Big Daddy's hand was a blur. The first shot took Scarface through his gun hand, sending his weapon spinning. The second caught the other rider in the shoulder as he cleared leather.

"Now boys," Big Daddy's voice remained pleasant, though his smoking Colt suggested otherwise, "I got two more rounds in this hogleg. Way I figure it, that's one for each knee you got left. Unless you'd prefer to deliver a message back to Morton?"

The unwounded rider tried to draw his second gun. Big Daddy's shot caught him in the chest, dropping him from his saddle. Scarface wheeled his horse, but the third shot knocked him clean off his mount.

"Shame," Big Daddy sighed, holstering his smoking gun. "Could have saved themselves a lot of trouble by just listening." He turned to his men. "Feed their horses, bury these two out by the north fence. And somebody fetch Doc Matthews — seems I might have nicked an artery on that last one."

He looked up at my window, tipping his hat. "Pardon the mess, Reverend. Been a while since I had to demonstrate proper manners to uninvited guests."

Sally clicked her tongue disapprovingly. "Always did have a peculiar way of handling social calls."

"Like you taught me, Sally," his booming laugh carried up. "Be polite, be professional, but have a plan to kill everybody you meet."

"That ain't what I taught you and you know it!" But there was a hint of pride in her voice.

Doc Matthews appeared below, medical bag in hand. "Dammit Lawrence, couldn't you have left at least one of them breathing? Getting tired of declaring time of death as my only medical opinion."

"Sorry Doc," Big Daddy grinned. "Guess I'm getting slow in my old age. Used to be able to wing 'em proper, just like you showed me during the war."

As his men cleaned up the courtyard, Big Daddy turned to Thomas, who hadn't moved from the stallion's side. "You alright, son?"

Thomas nodded, calm as could be. "Horse says there's more coming. At least six, from the west."

Big Daddy's eyebrows shot up. "That so? Well now, ain't that interesting." He looked back up at my window.

"Reverend, might want to stay put up there. Seems we're about to have us a proper reception committee."

As Big Daddy's men cleared the courtyard, Sally helped me back to bed, her face troubled. "There's something you need to know," she said quietly. "Something about what your Michelle really found."

She pulled a worn leather journal from her apron pocket. "This was in that book your wife had. Big Daddy didn't want to show you yet, thought you weren't strong enough. But with Morton's men showing up…" She handed me the journal. "You need to know what you're really fighting against."

The journal's pages were filled with neat columns of names, dates, and numbers. At first glance, it looked like a business ledger. Then I saw what the entries really meant.

"During the war," Sally's voice was heavy, "Thompson and Morton didn't just work for the army. They had a side business. Would find women – especially ones with special gifts or beautiful daughters – and sell them to fancy houses in New Orleans, Memphis, even up North."

My hands shook as I read. Each entry represented a family destroyed, women sold into bondage, children who'd "disappeared."

"Your Michelle," Sally continued, "she figured it out. Found proof they never stopped after the war. Just got more careful about it. Thompson would use his position as deacon to identify targets. Morton would do the killing. They had a whole network – judges who'd declare the women unfit mothers, doctors who'd certify deaths, brothel owners who'd pay top dollar for girls with special talents."

The last pages were In Michelle's handwriting. She'd traced the pattern back thirty years – hundreds of families targeted, women sold, children vanished. All connected to Thompson and Morton's operation.

"That's why they really came after your family," Big Daddy's voice came from the doorway. He filled the frame, his usual joviality gone. "Michelle wasn't just gathering evidence about land fraud. She found their whole operation. Found the brothels where they're still keeping women. Found the graves of the families they've killed. Even found some of the missing children."

"And Grace?" My voice was barely a whisper. "The other children?"

"Morton wasn't just after revenge," Big Daddy said grimly. "Girl like Grace, with healing in her hands? They got buyers who'd pay a fortune for that. Rachel's mind, Thomas's gift with animals – they sell special talents to special clients. Rich men who collect people with abilities, like they collect paintings or horses."

A sound from the courtyard drew us to the window. More riders were approaching – at least six, just as Thomas had sensed.

"Difference is," Big Daddy's hand moved to his gun, "this time they picked the wrong family to target. Your Michelle made sure of that when she sent copies of everything to people like me. People who've been waiting years to bring down Thompson's network."

He turned to me, his massive frame blocking the light. "That's the real reason you're here, Reverend. Not just to heal up. Your family is the key to destroying their whole operation. Living proof of what they've been doing all these years." Gunfire erupted from below.

"Now then," Big Daddy checked his weapon, "seems like Morton's friends have arrived. Might be time to show them what happens when they try to take children from my house."

A dozen riders appeared at the gate, led by a man I recognized as Reed, one of Thompson's old associates.

"Well butter my backside and call me a biscuit," Big Daddy boomed, rising from his creaking chair. "If it ain't Timothy Reed. Still wearing that same ugly hat from the war, I see."
"Lawrence," Reed called out. "Looking... large as ever."
"And you're looking about as smart as a soup sandwich, bringing guns to my property."

Big Daddy turned to Doc Matthews. "You steady enough to shoot, or you just gonna bore them to death with your war stories?"

Doc took a long pull from his flask. "I'll have you know I'm an excellent shot. Though..." he squinted at the riders, "when did they start sending triplets on raids?"
"Those ain't triplets, you old fool," Big Daddy laughed. "That's the whiskey talking. Just try not to shoot me – ain't easy to miss something my size, but you'd probably manage it."

Reed's men spread out, guns drawn. "Last chance, Lawrence. Hand over the children."
"Now see," Big Daddy sighed dramatically, "you done gone and interrupted my coffee time. Sally just made a fresh pot too."

He looked at Doc. "You take the six on the right?

"There's only five on the right," Doc squinted.

"No, there's definitely six."

"Well, one of them's awful blurry..."

"Just shoot the ones pointing guns at us!"
The firefight that followed was almost comical. Big Daddy moved with surprising grace for his size, his massive rifle barking death while he provided running commentary.

"That's for tracking mud on Sally's clean porch!" BOOM!

"That's for making me miss my coffee!" BOOM!

"And that's just because your horse looks stupid!"

Meanwhile, Doc Matthews stumbled around the porch, somehow managing to hit his targets despite seeing double

. "Stand still, you blurry bastards! No, not you Lawrence – though there seem to be three of you now…"

"There's only one of me, you drunken fool!"
"Well that's a mercy – world ain't ready for more than one of you."

Reed tried to flank them but slipped in a puddle of spilled whiskey from Doc's flask. Big Daddy's laugh shook the windows as he drew down on him.

"Now Reed," he called out jovially, "I got two questions for you.

First, you ever seen a man my size move this fast?"

Reed's eyes widened. "What's the second question?"

"How's that bullet hole feeling?"
BOOM!

When the smoke cleared, twelve bodies lay scattered across Sally's courtyard. Doc Matthews stumbled triumphantly across the porch, tripped over his own feet, and landed face-first in a flower pot.

"I meant to do that," came his muffled voice. "Was checking Sally's petunias for bullet holes."
"Only holes round here are in your head," Sally appeared with a fresh coffee pot. "And in my clean courtyard. Again."

"Now Sally," Big Daddy grinned, helping Doc up, "least they had the courtesy to die in neat piles this time."
"I helped!" Doc declared proudly, his hat askew and face covered in dirt.

"Yes you did," Big Daddy patted his shoulder. "Even if you was seeing two of everybody."

"Three," Doc corrected, brushing potting soil from his beard. "Was seeing three of everybody. Made it easier to hit at least one of them."

Sally just shook her head. "Lord save me from men who think gunfights are social occasions. Now, you want this coffee or should I just pour it on the bodies to wake them up?"

The sun was setting over Big Daddy's estate, painting the bloodstained courtyard in shades of amber and gold. Sally emerged onto the porch, coffee pot in one hand and medical kit in the other, surveying the carnage with a resigned expression.

"Lawrence Watkins," she scolded, tending to a small graze on Big Daddy's massive arm, "what have I told you about getting blood on my clean porch?"

"Now Sally," Big Daddy's laugh boomed across the yard, "ain't my fault they chose to die in such untidy places."

Doc Matthews stumbled up the steps, his face still covered in potting soil from his earlier encounter with Sally's flower bed. "I'll have you know I killed at least four of them. Or maybe it was two… they kept moving around too much."

"Only thing you killed was my petunias," Sally muttered. "That flower pot attacked me without provocation!" Doc declared, attempting to dust himself off but mostly just rearranging the dirt. "Besides, I meant to fall into those flowers. Was a tactical decision."

"Only tactical thing about you right now is how you manage to find every obstacle between here and that whiskey flask," Big Daddy chuckled. "Speaking of which…" He pulled out his pocket watch. "Sally, ain't it time for Doc's medicine?"

"Lord help me," Sally threw up her hands. "You two are worse than schoolboys. Got twelve dead men in my yard and you're making jokes."

"Thirteen," Doc corrected proudly. "That last fellow fell into your rose bushes."

"That was you, you old fool," Big Daddy's laugh shook the windows. "Not ten minutes ago."

I emerged onto the porch then, my children close beside me. Despite the violence we'd witnessed, seeing these three bickering like family brought a measure of peace. Rachel and Grace settled into rocking chairs while Thomas leaned against a pillar, watching the sunset.

"Speaking of fools," Sally said suddenly, "ain't it time we showed them what's in that lockbox, Lawrence?"

Before Big Daddy could respond, hoofbeats approached. Four riders appeared at the gate – Marshal Jenkins and his deputies, right on schedule.

"Lawrence," the Marshal nodded, taking in the scattered bodies. "I see you've been…entertaining."

"Just some uninvited guests who wouldn't take no for an answer," Big Daddy smiled pleasantly. "Sally, might want to take the children inside while we discuss business with the Marshal."

After Sally ushered my children away with promises of fresh biscuits, we men gathered in Big Daddy's study. The massive oak desk was covered with papers from the lockbox – ledgers, receipts, photographs spanning twenty years.

"Started during the war," Big Daddy explained, his jovial manner gone.

"Thompson and Morton would identify vulnerable women through refugee camps. Sell them to brothels in New Orleans, St. Louis, even Chicago. After the war, they got more organized. Used the church to find targets. Morton would arrange 'accidents' for the families, then they'd sell the women and children through their 'adoption agency.'"

The evidence was damning - detailed records of transactions, prices paid, properties acquired through murder and fraud. My hands shook as I recognized names of women who'd disappeared from neighboring parishes over the years.

"That's what Michelle discovered," Doc Matthews said quietly, flask forgotten. "Found their whole operation laid out. Must've been gathering evidence for months before they killed her."

"Operation's still running," Big Daddy added grimly. "Even with Thompson dead. Got friends in high places – judges, bankers, men who've profited from this evil for decades."

Marshal Jenkins studied the papers. "This is enough to hang everyone involved. But Morton's still out there…"
"Not for long," Big Daddy stood, his massive frame casting long shadows in the lamplight. "Reverend, I reckon it's time we went hunting. Doc here'll ride with us – assuming he can stay on a horse."

"I'll have you know I'm an excellent rider," Doc protested. "When the ground stops moving."

"I'll watch over your little ones," Sally said from the doorway. "Keep them safe while you do what needs doing."

My children were waiting on the porch when I went to say goodbye. Thomas stood straight and tall, becoming a man before his time. Rachel held Grace's hand, both trying to be brave.

"I'll come back," I promised, holding them close. "Going to find Morton, make him answer for what he did to your mama and our family. Some evils in this world need to be answered with righteousness."

"And bullets," Big Daddy added from behind me. "Lots of bullets."

"Best we leave at first light," Big Daddy said, his massive frame silhouetted against the setting sun. "Doc, you think you can sober up by then?"

"Bold of you to assume I plan to sober up at all," Doc Matthews grinned, finally managing to clean some of the dirt from his face. "Besides, I shoot better with my special medicine."

"Only because you see three targets and one of them's bound to be real," Big Daddy chuckled. "Sally, we'll need provisions for about a week's ride."

"Already packing them," Sally nodded. "Though knowing you two, I better include extra medical supplies and enough of Doc's 'medicine' to keep him from going through the shakes."

"Now see here," Doc drew himself up with exaggerated dignity, "I'm a professional man of medicine!"
"Professional at falling down, maybe," Big Daddy's laugh boomed across the yard. "Speaking of which, someone might want to fish his hat out of that flower pot before we leave."

I held my children close one last time, memorizing their faces. Thomas, trying so hard to be strong. Rachel, her mother's determination in her eyes. Little Grace, fighting back tears.

"How will you find him?" Thomas asked quietly.
"Morton's got a pattern," Big Daddy answered before I could. "Man like that, running from a bullet wound, he'll head for familiar ground. Got friends watching every brothel and gambling house from here to New Orleans. He shows his face, we'll know." "And then?" Rachel's voice was small but steady.

"Then," I said softly, "we make sure he can never hurt another family like he hurt ours."
"Just stay away from my flower beds when you do it," Sally muttered, but her eyes were kind. "Come on now, children.

Let's get you inside before these old fools start telling war stories."

"Old?" Big Daddy protested. "I'm in my prime!"

"Your prime was twenty years and two hundred pounds ago," Doc shot back.

"At least I can still see straight," Big Daddy grinned. "Unlike some doctors I could name."

"I see perfectly fine," Doc declared, walking straight into a porch column. "That pillar moved on its own and you know it."

As their bickering faded into the house, I stood alone on the porch, watching the last light fade from the sky. Somewhere out there, Morton was hiding, nursing his wounds and plotting revenge. But he didn't know what was coming for him. Didn't know that this time, the shepherd wasn't just protecting his flock – he was hunting wolves.

"We'll leave at dawn," Big Daddy's voice came from behind me, serious now. "Doc's loading the rifles, and Sally's got food enough for a small army – which, considering my appetite, we might need."

I nodded, touching Michelle's Bible in my pocket. "Thank you. Both of you. For everything."

"Ain't nothing to thank us for," he replied. "Some evils need answering. Besides," his usual grin returned, "been a while since Doc and I had a proper adventure. Though Lord help us all if he tries to ride a horse in his current state."

"I heard that!" Doc's voice carried from inside. "And I'll have you know I'm perfectly capable of… ow! Sally, who moved this doorway?"

Big Daddy's laugh echoed across the darkening yard. "Get some rest, Reverend. Tomorrow, we ride. And may God have mercy on Morton's soul, 'cause we sure ain't planning to."

CHAPTER 6: THE SHEPHERD'S RECKONING

'

Three men rode into Rising Sun, Texas just as the morning heat began to shimmer off the dusty street. The massive figure of Big Daddy Watkins led the way, his huge war horse straining under his weight. Doc Matthews swayed slightly in his saddle, though whether from his 'medicine' or the early hour was hard to tell. Behind them, Victor
Wright rode silent as a shadow, his preacher's collar replaced by a gunfighter's rig.

"Now this here," Big Daddy announced, his voice carrying across the empty street, "is what Sally calls a 'den of iniquity.

 Course, that might just be because last time we was here, Doc tried to marry a cactus."

"That cactus," Doc protested with dignity, "was a perfect lady. And I was only proposing because someone," he glared at Big Daddy,

"told me she was a wealthy widow."

"Ain't my fault you can't tell the difference between a plant and a person after eight drinks."

"It was only six drinks.

 The other two were purely medicinal."

The town was just waking up, shopkeepers sweeping dust from wooden sidewalks, saloon girls making their weary way home. Two weeks of hard riding had brought them here, following Morton's trail of blood and borrowed horses. The brothel owner in Shreveport had talked freely enough once Big Daddy explained things to him. The farmer's wife outside Dallas remembered treating a man with bullet wounds who matched Morton's description. And now Rising Sun, where Thompson had started his operation during the war.

"What do you make of them riders watching us from the livery?" Big Daddy asked casually, not turning his head. "Three of them," Doc replied, suddenly sounding considerably more sober.

"Unless I'm seeing double again, in which case maybe six."

"Four," Victor spoke for the first time that morning.

"One by the water trough, two in the shadows, one on the roof with a rifle."

"Well now," Big Daddy's massive frame straightened in his saddle. "Ain't that interesting? Reckon Morton's expecting company?"

"Man's been running two weeks with two bullet holes in him," Doc observed. "Bound to get paranoid. Speaking of which..." He reached for his flask.

"You really need that medicine right now?" Big Daddy asked.

"Way I see it," Doc took a long pull, "either I'm right about them being Morton's men and we're about to have some excitement, or I'm wrong and I just had a nice morning drink. Either way, I win."

They rode on, past the shuttered general store, past the saloon with its weathered sign.
The church at the end of the street had been converted into something else years ago – window glass painted black, cross removed from the steeple. A sign hung over the door: "The Pearly Gates."

"Ain't that just like Morton," Big Daddy spat. "Turn a house of God into a house of sin."

"Speaking of sin," Doc nodded toward the livery, "our friends are getting restless."

The watching men had emerged from hiding, guns plain on their hips. Their leader, a scarred man with a Texas Rangers star that was probably stolen, stepped into the street.

"This here's a private town, gentlemen," he called out. "Might want to ride on through."

"Might want to," Big Daddy agreed pleasantly. "Ain't going to, but it's a nice thought." His massive frame seemed to expand somehow. "Now why don't you boys run tell James Morton that some old friends have come to visit? Man with two bullet holes in him? Ring any bells?"

The scarred man's hand dropped to his gun. "Don't know any Morton."
"That's funny,"

Doc Matthews took another drink. "'Cause either I'm seeing double, or that's his horse in your stable. The one with the distinctive Mexican saddle and bloodstains on the blanket."

"Last chance," the scarred man warned. "Ride out now, or—"

What happened next moved almost too fast to follow. Despite his enormous size, Big Daddy's hand was a blur.

The scarred man's gun had barely cleared leather when Big Daddy's shot took him in the shoulder, spinning him around. The other three went for their weapons, but Doc's scatter gun boomed twice, and suddenly the street was very empty.

"Well," Doc observed cheerfully, reloading, "reckon Morton knows we're here now."

"Reckon so," Big Daddy agreed. He turned to Victor. "You ready for this, Reverend?

Man we're hunting ain't just some wounded animal. He's got friends here, men who've profited from his evil for years."

Victor checked his guns with steady hands, feeling the weight of Michelle's Bible in his coat. Two weeks of riding had burned away any hesitation, any doubt. This wasn't about revenge anymore. This was about justice. About answering evil with righteousness.

"Let's finish this," he said quietly.

Big Daddy's grin was fierce in the morning light.

 "Doc? You steady enough to handle some more excitement?"

"Long as nobody expects me to marry any more cacti,"

Doc Matthews straightened in his saddle. "Though I got to admit, that one in Shreveport was kind of pretty…"

"Now then," Big Daddy dismounted, his massive frame making the boardwalk groan. "How do you gentlemen want to handle this?"

"Could try asking politely," Doc suggested, nearly missing the ground as he slid from his saddle. "Though last time I tried being polite in a brothel, I woke up married to a goat."

"That wasn't a goat," Big Daddy chuckled. "That was the mayor's wife."

"Explains why she ate my hat."

Victor shook his head, a faint smile touching his lips despite the gravity of their purpose. "You two ever going to tell a story that doesn't end with Doc marrying something?"

"Now that ain't fair," Doc protested. "Sometimes the stories end with Big Daddy sitting on somebody. Speaking of which…" He nodded toward The Pearly Gates, where more armed men had appeared.

"Eight of them," Big Daddy observed casually.

"Unless Doc's seeing double again, in which case maybe four."

"Ten," Victor corrected, checking his guns. "Two on the balcony with rifles."

"Twelve," Doc added proudly. "Though them last two might be the whiskey talking."

"Lord help us," Victor muttered. "I'm about to storm a brothel with a giant who can't count and a doctor who's seeing double."

"Triple," Doc corrected helpfully. "And I'll have you know my medical condition is purely professional."

"Only thing professional about you is how often you fall down," Big Daddy laughed.

Then, raising his voice: "Morning, boys! Don't suppose you'd believe we're here for the Sunday service?"

"Place ain't been a church in twenty years," one of the men called back.

"Well now," Victor stepped forward, his voice carrying the authority of his former calling,

"might be time to reconsecrate it. Right after we have a word with James Morton."

"Ain't no Morton here!"

"That's funny," Doc took a contemplative sip from his flask. "'Cause either I'm drunker than usual, or that's his blood trail leading right up them stairs."

"Could be anybody's blood," another man argued.

"Nope," Big Daddy's massive hand rested on his gun.

"Morton bleeds exactly like what he is – a snake. Now, you boys can step aside, or you can find out why they used to call me The Mountain That Moves."

"I thought they called you that 'cause you ate like one," Doc mused.

"That was later. After Sally's cooking."

"Speaking of Sally," Victor added dryly, "she made me promise not to let either of you get blood on your clean shirts. Something about being tired of patching bullet holes."

"Way I see it," Big Daddy grinned, "long as we leave one of them alive to do the laundry, we're keeping our word." The men on the porch shifted nervously, clearly not used to people who joked in the face of their threats. Their leader, a thin man with a cavalry mustache, stepped forward.

"This here's your last warning…"

"No," Victor's voice cut through the morning air like a blade. "This here's yours. James Morton killed my wife, orphaned my children, and has spent twenty years selling women and children into bondage. Now either you step aside, or we'll find out if Doc here can still practice medicine with broken fingers."

"That's assuming I can find their fingers in all this dust," Doc squinted. "Everything's a bit blurry at the moment." "Everything's been blurry since 1863," Big Daddy reminded him.

"That was a tactical decision. Harder to treat wounded soldiers when you can see how ugly they are."

The thin man's hand dropped to his gun. Time seemed to slow, like it always did in moments before violence.

"You know," Victor said conversationally, "my wife always said there were two types of fools in this world – those who don't know any better, and those who do." "And which type are we?"

Doc asked, casually adjusting his grip on his scatter gun.

"Oh, definitely the second kind," Big Daddy grinned. "Sally reminds me every Sunday."

The first shot came from the balcony – a clean miss that kicked up dust between Victor's feet. What followed was pure chaos.

Big Daddy moved with impossible speed for his size, his massive frame somehow diving behind a water trough while drawing and firing in one motion. Two men fell before they could clear leather.

"Hot damn!" Doc whooped, his scatter gun booming. "I love it when they stand in groups of three! Makes it easier to hit the real one!"

"There's only two of them, you old fool!" Big Daddy called back.

"Not from where I'm standing!"

"You ain't standing, you're lying in Sally's flower bed again!"

"These ain't flowers," Doc protested from behind an overturned cart. "These is… tactical vegetation."

Victor's guns seemed to fire themselves, muscle memory from his gunslinger days taking over. Three more men fell, their shots going wild. "If you two are done discussing botany…"

"Always did like them fancy words of yours, Reverend," Big Daddy laughed, reloading with practiced ease. "Almost makes getting shot at sound educational."

A bullet sparked off the water trough near Big Daddy's head. He responded by picking up the entire trough and throwing it at the shooter, water, wood, and all.

"Now that," Doc observed, pausing to take a drink mid-firefight, "is what Sally means by 'unnecessary showing off.'"

"Ain't showing off if you hit what you're aiming at," Big Daddy protested. "Besides, man my size has to make his own cover."

"Speaking of cover," Victor cut in, "either of you gentlemen care to handle those fellows on the balcony? They're making it difficult to have a proper conversation." "I got them!" Doc declared, raising his scatter gun.

"No!" Both Victor and Big Daddy shouted together. "Last time you shot high, you killed three chickens and married a weather vane," Big Daddy reminded him. "That weather vane had it coming," Doc muttered, but lowered his gun.

The Pearly Gates erupted in gunfire as the three men advanced. Big Daddy's massive frame somehow moved from cover to cover with surprising grace, though the barrels he ducked behind looked comically small against his bulk.

"You know," he called out between shots, "this reminds me of that time in Shreveport when Doc tried to arrest his own reflection!"

"That mirror was giving me suspicious looks!" Doc protested, reloading his scatter gun. "Besides, I won that fight!"

"You shot up a saloon mirror and tried to put handcuffs on broken glass," Victor reminded him, picking off another shooter from the balcony.

"Still counts as a victory. Mirror ain't never looked at me wrong again."

They pushed forward through the gunsmoke, working their way toward the converted church's entrance. A man burst through the swinging doors with a shotgun, only to find himself face-to-belly with Big Daddy.

"Well now," Big Daddy looked down at him. "Ain't you just a bit short for this line of work?"

Before the man could respond, Big Daddy simply picked him up and tossed him through the window of the general store across the street.

"Lawrence Watkins!" Victor called in his best preacher voice. "What would Sally say about throwing people through windows?"

"She'd say I better not expect her to clean up the mess," Big Daddy chuckled. "Speaking of messes… Doc, you planning on getting up from behind that horse trough anytime soon?"

"I'll have you know," Doc's voice came indignantly from his cover, "I am conducting a thorough medical examination of this trough's construction. Also, I appear to be stuck."

A fresh volley of bullets interrupted their banter. Three more of Morton's men had taken position in the saloon across the way, laying down covering fire while others tried to flank them.

"Don't suppose either of you gentlemen have a plan?" Victor asked, ducking behind a pillar.

"I always got a plan," Big Daddy grinned. "Doc, you still got that bottle of whiskey you've been saving?"

"My emergency medical supplies? What kind of doctor would I be without… wait." Doc's eyes narrowed suspiciously.

"What are you planning to do with my medicine?"

"Remember that trick we learned during the war? The one with the bottle and the…"

"Oh no," Doc clutched his flask protectively. "Last time we tried that, you singed off half your beard and I lost my favorite hat!"

"To be fair," Victor interjected, "you lose your hat at least twice a week anyway."

"That's entirely different! Those hats run away on their own accord. Especially after I've had my medicine."

"Fine," Doc finally surrendered his precious whiskey bottle.

"But if this goes like Shreveport, you're explaining to Sally why we're missing eyebrows again."

Big Daddy's grin was downright alarming as he stuffed a rag in the bottle. "Reverend, might want to say a quick prayer for our friends in the saloon."

"Pretty sure the Good Lord ain't interested in this kind of prayer," Victor replied dryly, but he couldn't help smiling as Big Daddy lit the rag.

The makeshift bomb sailed through the air in a perfect arc – surprisingly delicate for something thrown by a man the size of a small house. It crashed through the saloon window, followed immediately by panicked shouts and a sizeable explosion.

"Hot damn!" Doc celebrated. "Did you see that? Actually, I'm seeing about three of that, and they're all spectacular!" "Less admiring, more moving," Victor urged, already pushing forward. "Morton's going to run if we give him the chance."

They fought their way into The Pearly Gates, through what had once been the church's main sanctuary. The pews had been replaced with gaming tables, the altar with a bar. The sight made Victor's blood boil.

"Now this here," Big Daddy announced, ducking under bullets while somehow still looking offended, "is just plain disrespectful to proper architecture. Look what they done to them stained glass windows!"

"I think the bullets flying through them ain't helping either," Doc observed helpfully, taking cover behind the bar. "Say, they got any medicine back here? For tactical purposes?"

"You ain't medicating yourself in the middle of a gunfight!" Big Daddy bellowed, picking up an entire poker table and using it as a shield.

"Watch me!" Doc reached for a bottle, then yelped as a bullet shattered it. "Now that's just uncivilized! Victor, these fellows need a sermon about wasting good liquor!"

"Pretty sure my preaching days are behind me," Victor called back, advancing steadily through the chaos.

Then he spotted a familiar figure at the top of the stairs. "Morton!"

James Morton, looking considerably worse for wear, fired wildly down at them before disappearing through a door.

"He's heading for the roof!"
Big Daddy shouted. "Doc, you take the back stairs

! Victor, go up the front! I'll…" He paused to throw
another poker table at a group of shooters.

"I'll make sure nobody follows you up!"

"You just want to stay near the bar," Doc accused,
staggering toward the back stairs.

"Somebody's got to make sure you don't try to marry it!"

Victor took the front stairs three at a time, driven by the
memory of Michelle's smile, of his lost children's laughter.
He burst onto the roof just in time to see Morton jumping
to the next building.

The chase led across rooftops, through windows, over
balconies. Below, Big Daddy and Doc followed at street
level, providing covering fire and colorful commentary.

"Did you see that jump?" Doc's voice carried up.

"Rather athletic for a man with two bullet holes!"

"Three now!" Big Daddy called back, his massive frame
somehow keeping pace despite his size. "Victor just added
another one!"

Morton finally made it to the stables, mounting a horse
and breaking for open country.

Victor's last shot clipped the man's ear just as he cleared the town limits.

"Well shit," Big Daddy puffed up beside Victor, who had run down to the street.

"Man rides like the devil's chasing him."

"Worse," Victor said grimly, checking his guns. "He's got a preacher after him."

"A preacher, a drunk doctor, and whatever the hell Big Daddy is," Doc added, finally catching up and taking a long pull from a new bottle he'd acquired somewhere in the chaos.

"Where'd you get that?" Big Daddy demanded.

"Tactical acquisition behind the bar. For medicinal purposes." Doc grinned.

"Also, I think I may have accidentally proposed to a hat rack during the excitement."

Victor studied the horizon where Morton had disappeared. "He's heading south. Toward Texas."

Big Daddy's usual jovial expression turned serious. "Guadalupe Pass?"
Victor nodded slowly.

"He's running back to where it all started. Back to that revival tent where I first met Michelle."

"Poetic," Doc observed. "In a bloody sort of way."

"Mount up," Victor said quietly, checking Michelle's Bible in his coat. "Time to end this where it began."

"Just one quick question," Doc raised his hand like a schoolboy. "Does anyone remember which of these horses is mine? They all keep moving around.
"

"Lord give me strength," Big Daddy muttered, lifting Doc bodily onto his saddle

"Victor, you sure you want us riding with you for this last part?"

"Wouldn't have it any other way," Victor allowed himself a small smile. "Though I'm starting to understand why Sally drinks."

They rode hard through the afternoon heat, following Morton's trail south. Big Daddy's massive frame somehow managed to keep his horse at a steady pace, despite looking like a mountain trying to ride a molehill. Doc swayed in his saddle, though he swore it was "tactical swaying" to confuse any pursuers.

"You know," Doc mused, pulling out his ever-present flask, "seems to me we're chasing an awful lot of memories along with Morton."

"Man's heading straight for Guadalupe Pass," Big Daddy nodded.

"Where you first met
Michelle, ain't it, Victor?"

Victor touched his wife's Bible, feeling its familiar weight. "That revival tent where she first came in, trying to hide her bruises. Where all this started."

"Fitting place to end it," Big Daddy's usual joviality was replaced with something harder

. "Though I got to wonder if Morton chose it on purpose. Man like that, he might have something planned."

"Only thing he's got planned is bleeding," Doc observed professionally. "Way he's riding, them bullet holes ain't healing clean. Course, I'm seeing two trails of blood, but I'm pretty sure one of them's the whiskey talking."
They made camp as darkness fell, though none of them slept much.

The weight of what lay ahead settled over them like a heavy blanket. Even Doc's usual chatter was subdued. "Victor," Big Daddy said quietly over the campfire, "you know tomorrow ain't just about killing Morton. It's about ending something bigger. Something that's been growing like poison since the war."

"I know," Victor stared into the flames.

"Michelle knew it too. That's why she kept digging, kept gathering evidence. She knew Morton and Thompson were just the visible part of it."

"Like a snake," Doc added, surprisingly lucid. "Cut off the head, but the body keeps writhing. Got to burn out the whole nest."

"That what we're doing?" Victor asked softly. "Burning out a nest of snakes?"

"We're answering evil with righteousness," Big Daddy's voice rumbled like distant thunder. "Like you preached about all them years. Sometimes that means using fire instead of scripture."

Dawn found them breaking camp, checking weapons, preparing for what lay ahead. The revival grounds where it all began were less than half a day's ride away.

"One last thing," Big Daddy pulled something massive from his saddlebag. "Sally sent this along. Said we might need it."

It was his old Civil War rifle, the one he'd used at Willow Grove. A weapon made for ending things.

"Also," Doc added, producing a bottle, "she sent this.

Said if we're fool enough to chase a madman across Texas, we might as well do it properly fortified."

"That woman," Big Daddy chuckled, "knows us too well."

They mounted up as the sun cleared the horizon. Victor checked his guns one last time, felt Michelle's Bible close to his heart. Twenty years of history was about to come full circle.

"Well gentlemen," Big Daddy's massive frame straightened in his saddle, "shall we go answer evil with righteousness?"

"And bullets," Doc added helpfully. "Lots of bullets."

"Amen to that," Victor said quietly, and they rode toward Guadalupe Pass, toward a final reckoning twenty years in the making.

CHAPTER 7: A TALE OF REDEMPTION

The old church at Guadalupe Pass stood silhouetted against the setting sun, its weathered cross casting a long shadow across ground that had once been holy. Twenty years had weathered its walls, but they still held the echo of hymns and hope, of a night when a frightened woman sought sanctuary from a monster wearing a man's face.

"Place looks different," Big Daddy muttered, studying the building through his field glasses.

"Quieter than a graveyard at midnight."

"Speaking of graveyards," Doc Matthews took a thoughtful pull from his flask, "anybody else notice them fresh horses behind the church? Unless I'm seeing double – which, mind you, is entirely possible – I count six."

"Eight," Victor corrected quietly, checking his guns. "Morton's gray stallion among them. Still got blood on the saddle blanket."

Big Daddy's massive frame somehow stayed concealed behind a boulder that should have been too small to hide him. "Man's been bleeding since Arkansas. Way he's riding, wound's got to be festering something fierce."

"Good," Victor said softly, touching Michelle's Bible in his coat. The pages were worn smooth from twenty years of her hands, stained with what he now knew was her blood from that final night.

"Now Reverend," Doc struggled to his feet, picking cactus needles from his coat, "don't suppose we could discuss this situation like civilized folk? Maybe over a bottle of my special medicine?"

"Last time we tried being civilized," Big Daddy reminded him, "you tried to deputize a water trough."

"That trough had suspicious intentions and you know it!"

Victor barely heard their banter. His eyes were fixed on the church window where he'd first seen Michelle all those years ago. She'd been so young, so frightened, yet somehow still strong enough to seek help. To believe in redemption.

"You know it's a trap," Big Daddy said finally, his usual joviality replaced with something harder.

"Morton picked this place special. Means to finish what he started."

"Man's got a peculiar sense of poetry," Doc observed, now somehow tangled in a new patch of cacti.

"Though I got to admit, these tactical desert plants are becoming personally offensive."

"Only thing offensive is watching you fight with a cactus," Big Daddy chuckled. "And losing."

"I ain't losing," Doc declared with dignity. "I'm conducting a strategic withdrawal from hostile vegetation." Victor checked his guns one final time.

 "Morton's in there. Two men in the bell tower, two by the front door. Probably more inside."

"So," Big Daddy's massive hands wrapped around his rifle, "how you want to play this?"

"Front door," Victor said quietly. "Let's answer evil right up the middle."

"Simple. Direct. Probably gonna get us killed." Big Daddy's grin was fierce in the fading light. "Sally's gonna be furious."

"She's always furious," Doc pointed out, finally extracting himself from the cacti. "Last week she was furious about me trying to marry that scarecrow."

"That was this morning, you old fool."
"Was it? Well, in my defense, it was a very well-dressed scarecrow."

They moved through the gathering darkness, three mismatched avengers approaching judgment. The setting sun painted the church in shades of blood and gold, turning the weathered cross into a finger pointing toward heaven – or perhaps marking the spot where twenty years of evil would finally meet its reckoning.

The church doors creaked open at Victor's touch, spilling lamplight onto the worn steps. Inside, the sanctuary looked like a mockery of what it had once been. Gaming tables were scattered among the remaining pews, empty bottles littered the floor where worshippers had once knelt in prayer.

"Well now," Big Daddy's voice echoed in the quiet space, "this here's what Sally would call 'a desperate need for housekeeping.'"

"And proper drinking etiquette," Doc added, studying the discarded bottles with professional disappointment.

"Perfectly good whiskey gone to waste. Though..." He squinted at the altar. "Either I'm seeing double, or there's an awful lot of rifles pointed our way."

"Gentlemen!" Morton's voice rang out from the shadows. "So kind of you to join us."

Men emerged from behind pillars and pews, guns trained steady. Morton himself stood at the altar, looking pale and sickly in the lamplight. Blood stained his left side where Victor's bullet had found him weeks ago.

"Drop your weapons," Morton commanded. "Unless you'd prefer a more direct path to heaven."

"Now see here," Big Daddy said pleasantly, his massive frame somehow making the church seem smaller, "way I was raised, it ain't polite to point guns in a house of God."

"This stopped being a house of God long ago," Morton sneered. "Rather fitting though, isn't it Victor? Ending things where they began?"

"Only thing fitting," Victor said quietly, "will be putting you in the ground."

"Brave words from a man about to die." Morton nodded to his men. "Take their guns. And be careful with the big one – he's faster than he looks."

"Speaking of looks," Doc Matthews swayed slightly, "anybody else notice how the floor keeps moving? Very disrespectful of church architecture if you ask me."

"That's the whiskey, you old fool," Big Daddy muttered as Morton's men relieved them of their weapons.

"Can't be the whiskey. I specifically labeled that flask

'Morton circled them slowly, enjoying his moment of triumph. "You see, Reverend, this was never about just one woman, or one piece of property. During the war, I discovered something far more valuable than cotton or cattle – the appetite of wealthy men for exotic merchandise."

"Merchandise?" Big Daddy's voice rumbled dangerously. "You mean people. Women and children."

"Products," Morton corrected, smiling coldly. "Carefully selected, properly conditioned. Do you know how much a beautiful woman with proper breeding is worth in certain circles? Or children from good families, raised to serve particular… tastes?"

Victor strained against his captors, but Morton's men held him firm.

"Your Michelle," Morton continued, "she was meant to be the centerpiece of my greatest deal. Ten million dollars from a consortium of buyers – judges, senators, even a governor or two. Not just for her, you understand, but for what she represented. Proof that even a respectable woman, a mother, could be… properly marketed."

"You're insane," Victor said quietly.

"Insane?" Morton laughed. "I built an empire! Thompson handled the church side, finding likely prospects through his ministry. I arranged the unfortunate accidents, cleared the properties. We had a perfect system. Until you…

" His face twisted. "Until you convinced her she was worth something more than her price tag."

"Man does love to hear himself talk," Doc observed woozily from the floor.

"Very inconsiderate to those of us with concussions."

"Shut up!" Morton kicked him. "You have no idea what you cost me. The deals that fell through. The buyers who lost confidence. Twenty years of building something magnificent, reduced to running discount brothels and penny-ante land grabs."

"Sounds to me like someone's bitter about their poor business acumen," Big Daddy said cheerfully.

"Maybe try selling something less likely to shoot back?"

Morton's gun cracked across Big Daddy's face, though the massive man barely flinched. "You think this is funny? I had senators in my pocket! Judges signing whatever papers I put in front of them! I was building a network that would have stretched from New Orleans to San Francisco!"

"And now," Victor said softly, "you're bleeding out in an abandoned church, trying to justify selling children to monsters."

"No," Morton's smile turned cruel. "Now I'm going to kill you slowly, just like I killed your precious Michelle. Then I'm going back to Arkansas to finish what I started with your remaining brats. The girl especially – Grace, isn't it? She'll fetch a fine price in certain markets…"
The mention of his daughter's name changed something in Victor's eyes. Even Morton took a step back from what he saw there.

"Speaking of corpses," Doc slurred from the floor, "anybody else notice how them fellows by the door keep looking mighty nervous at that smoke coming under it?"
Morton spun toward the entrance just as Big Daddy made his move. The massive man's chains snapped like thread as he lunged forward, grabbing the nearest guard and throwing him bodily into two others.

The man sailed through the air like a rag doll, crashing into the church's back wall with a sound like thunder.

"Hot damn!" Doc rolled behind a pew as gunfire erupted. "Either I'm seeing double, or Big Daddy just turned three men into flying lessons!"

"Ain't got time for your medicine talk!" Big Daddy roared, using another guard as a human shield while charging toward the altar. "Victor, get down!"

Victor dropped and rolled as bullets splintered the wood around him. His hands found a fallen gun, muscle memory from his gunslinger days taking over. Two quick shots dropped the men who'd been holding him.
Morton scrambled for cover behind the altar, screaming orders. "Kill them! Kill them all!"

"Now that's just rude," Big Daddy commented, picking up an entire pew and using it as a battering ram. "Sally's gonna be mighty upset about all this violence in a house of God."

"Sally's gonna be upset about what you're doing to that nice church furniture!" Doc called out, somehow having acquired both a gun and a fresh bottle during the chaos. The firefight turned the sanctuary into hell. Bullets splintered wood and shattered the remaining windows.

Big Daddy moved like a force of nature, his massive frame somehow dodging shots while dealing out destruction. Doc, despite his apparent drunkenness, dropped two men with surgical precision.

"You know what this reminds me of?" Doc shouted over the gunfire. "That time in Shreveport when Big Daddy tried to arrest that bear!"

"That weren't a bear," Big Daddy grunted, using his pew shield to smash through Morton's remaining men. "That was your reflection in a store window!"

"Was it? Well, in my defense, it was a very aggressive reflection!"

Victor moved steadily forward, each shot finding its mark. This wasn't revenge anymore - this was justice, pure and terrible. Morton's men fell one by one until only their leader remained, cornered behind the altar like a rat in a trap
.

Then Morton's lucky shot caught Victor in the shoulder, spinning him around. Another bullet took him in the leg. The third hit him in the chest, and the world went sideways.

"Victor!" Big Daddy's roar seemed to shake the whole church.

"I'm fine," Doc announced from somewhere, "thanks for asking! Though I appear to be shot. Unless..." He peered at his bloody arm. "No, definitely shot. Very inconsiderate of them."

Through blood-blurred vision, Victor watched Morton emerge from behind the bullet-riddled altar. Big Daddy lay wounded near the church doors, his massive frame finally stilled by two rounds to his chest. Doc wasn't moving at all, sprawled among the broken pews with his faithful flask still clutched in one hand.

"Look at them now," Morton gloated, limping closer. "Your mountain of a friend, bleeding out on consecrated ground. Your drunk doctor, finally silent. And you..." He smiled cruelly. "You're right where I've wanted you for twenty years."

Victor tried to raise his gun, but his arm wouldn't respond. The bullet in his shoulder had done more damage than he'd thought. Blood pooled beneath him, turning the ancient floorboards crimson
.

"You know what's funny?" Morton continued, clearly savoring the moment. "After I kill you, I'm going back for your children. Especially that sweet little Grace. The buyers in Shanghai are particularly interested in young ones with... special qualities."

"You ain't... touching my children," Victor managed through gritted teeth.

"And who's going to stop me? You? Look at you - the righteous preacher, bleeding out in his own church." Morton raised his pistol. "Any last words before I send you to meet your dear Michelle?"

The smoke that Doc had been warning about all evening was thicker now, curling under the door in dark waves. Morton didn't seem to notice, too focused on his moment of triumph.

"Actually," a voice said from behind him – a voice that stopped Victor's heart. "He ain't the one who needs last words."

Morton began to turn, his face showing the first hint of fear.

"Rot in hell, you son of a bitch."

The gunshot was deafening in the enclosed space. Morton's eyes went wide as red bloomed across his chest. He looked down at the wound in surprise, then at the figure standing behind him.

Michelle Wright stood in the smoke like an avenging angel, her gun still raised, her face illuminated by the flames now visible through the church windows.

"That's... impossible," Morton gasped. "I killed you..."
"You tried," Michelle's voice was steel. "Just like you tried to kill my family. To steal my children. But evil men like you..." She fired again, the bullet taking Morton in the throat. "You never could understand what a mother's love is capable of."

Morton fell, his blood mixing with Victor's on the church floor. His last breath came out as a gurgle, his eyes fixed on the cross above the altar.

"Michelle?" Victor's voice was barely a whisper.
She was at his side in an instant, pressing her hands against his wounds. "I'm here, my love. I've always been here.

Watching, waiting, gathering evidence against their whole network."
"But... how?"

"Later," she promised, tears mixing with the blood on her hands. "Right now we need to get you all out of here. I set fires at both exits - it's how we used to trap raiders during the war. This whole place is about to burn."

"Anybody else," Big Daddy's voice came weakly from the door, "smell something burning? Or is that just Doc's medicine finally catching up with me?"

"It's definitely catching up with somebody," Doc mumbled from his pew. "Though I got to admit, either I'm seeing double, or there's two Mrs. Wrights. In which case..." He tried to straighten his bloody coat. "Ma'am. Mams. Lovely evening for a resurrection"

"As much as I'd love to explain everything," Michelle said, helping Victor to his feet, "this church is about to become a very holy fire."

"Speaking of holy," Doc struggled upright, still clutching his flask, "I do believe I'm seeing angels. Unless…" He squinted at Michelle. "You wouldn't happen to be related to that windmill I nearly married in Shreveport?"

"That was a water pump, you old fool," Big Daddy groaned, his massive frame somehow managing to stand despite his wounds.

"And it was yesterday."

"Was it? Time does fly when you're getting shot."

The flames were spreading fast now, eating through the dry wood of the old church. Michelle guided them toward the back door, moving with the sure knowledge of someone who'd planned this moment carefully.

"I've got horses waiting," she said, supporting Victor's weight. "And before you ask – yes, I've been following you since Arkansas. Watching, gathering evidence, making sure every piece of their network was documented."

"You knew?" Victor's voice was weak from blood loss. "All this time?"

"Had to play dead," she explained, helping him onto a horse. "Had to let them think they'd won while I tracked down every connection, every corrupt official, every brothel and auction house in their operation."

"Very elaborate," Doc observed, somehow mounting his horse backward. "Though I got to ask – is the church supposed to be doing that?"

The old building was fully engulfed now, flames reaching toward heaven like prayers of judgment. As they rode clear, the steeple collapsed in a shower of sparks, the cross falling last into the inferno.

"Shame about the church," Big Daddy rumbled, his massive frame making his horse look like a pony. "Sally's gonna be mighty upset about us burning down another house of God."

"Another?" Michelle raised an eyebrow.

"Long story," Doc waved his flask dismissively. "Involves a very flammable baptism and some unnecessarily judgmental chickens."

They rode through the night, Michelle leading them to a hidden camp where she had medical supplies waiting. As she tended their wounds, she explained everything. "The neighbor who pulled me from the fire… he died going back in for the children.

That's the body they found. I was already gone by then, taken in by a network of women – others who'd escaped Morton and Thompson's operation. We've been working for years, documenting everything, building a case."

"The women's network Michelle used to help," Victor remembered. "The ones who maintained the safe houses…"

"All survivors," she nodded. "Women who'd lost everything to their evil. We've got evidence now – ledgers, letters, witness statements. Enough to bring down judges, politicians, bankers… their whole corrupt empire."

"Well now," Big Daddy managed a pained grin, "ain't that just the kind of news that calls for some of Doc's medicine?"

"Way ahead of you," Doc raised his flask triumphantly, then frowned. "Though I appear to be seeing three of everyone. Very inconsiderate of them to multiply without warning."

The following weeks saw justice fall like summer lightning across three states. Michelle's evidence, combined with Thompson's records and Morton's death, broke open a corruption network two decades in the making.

"Fourteen judges," Big Daddy read from the newspaper, his massive frame making the chair in his study groan. "Twenty-six politicians, and enough bankers to start their own town. Not bad for a woman they thought was dead."

"The Shanghai connection was the key," Michelle explained, pouring coffee for the wounded men. "Once we proved American officials were selling children overseas, even their friends in high places couldn't protect them."

"Speaking of protection,

" Doc wobbled in, arm in a sling, "Sally says if you don't stop pulling your stitches, Big Daddy, she's going to tie you to the bed."

"Woman's been threatening that since I was twelve," Big Daddy chuckled. "Though I notice you ain't mentioned your own healing process."

"That's because my medicine—"

"Is the reason Sally had to lock up all her curtain rods," Michelle interrupted with a smile. "After you tried to marry three of them. In one night."

"In my defense," Doc drew himself up with dignity, "those curtain rods were giving me very meaningful looks."

Victor sat quietly, watching his wife move through the room. Two weeks of proper care had done wonders for their wounds, but he still sometimes feared he'd wake to find this all a dream. Michelle must have sensed his thoughts, because she paused to squeeze his shoulder. "The children will be here tomorrow," she said softly. "Sarah's bringing them by wagon. All three of them, safe and sound."

"Speaking of sound," Big Daddy's voice turned serious, "there's something we need to discuss. About what Michelle found in California."

The room grew quiet. Even Doc set down his flask. "Thompson and Morton weren't the only ones running these operations," Michelle pulled out a final set of papers. "There's another network, bigger than theirs, operating out of San Francisco. They're the ones who wanted our Grace so badly."

"Then I reckon," Victor said quietly, "we've got more work to do."

"We?" Big Daddy raised an eyebrow. "You planning on dragging my old bones across more states, Reverend?" "Only if Doc promises not to marry any more plants along the way," Michelle smiled.

"That cactus," Doc protested, "sent me very clear signals!" The next day, three children flew down Big Daddy's front steps into their parents' arms. There were tears and laughter, questions and answers, and the kind of healing that only love can bring.

Thomas stood tall and proud, every inch his father's son. Rachel's sharp eyes missed nothing, especially the way her mother's hand never left her father's. And Grace… Grace simply glowed with joy.

But later that night, after the children were asleep, Victor found Michelle on the porch, staring west.
"You're thinking about California," he said softly.
She nodded. "There are more children out there, Victor. More families being destroyed. What we ended here… it's just the beginning."

"Then we'll finish it," he promised. "Together this time."
Inside, they could hear Big Daddy and Doc arguing about whether Doc had actually tried to propose to a wagon wheel that morning, or if it had proposed to him. Sally's voice rose above them both, threatening them with everything from bed rest to marriage counseling for the wagon wheel.

"You know," Michelle smiled, "with friends like these, we might just have a chance."

"More than a chance," Victor pulled her close. "We have righteousness on our side."

"And bullets," Doc called from inside. "Don't forget the bullets!"

"And my size!" Big Daddy added.

"And my medicine!"
"Lord help us all," Sally's voice drifted out.

"They're planning another adventure."

The sun set on Big Daddy's estate, painting the sky in colors of promise and warning. Somewhere to the west, evil men were building empires of suffering.

But they didn't know what was coming for them – a preacher who'd found his true calling, a wife back from the dead, and the most unlikely pair of allies any righteous cause ever had.

The war wasn't over...

But this time,
they'd fight it together.

Made in the USA
Columbia, SC
13 February 2025

53660489R00133